"As a current business consultant, former graduate school dean, and Ph.D. in Organizational Leadership, I am delighted to draw upon the professional and spiritual insights in Griffith Lindell's latest book, *Mastering a Servant-Leader Attitude*. The book integrates a survey of sound leader theory with transformational Christian applications. It is a ready inspirational reference for the business professional and a solid resource for the emerging leader or student entering into any profession. In changing the concepts of servant-leadership into "serving-leader" terms, Lindell activates the verb and translates theory into action. Lindell's work here is clearly grounded in a life of practical experience in leading others in business and building leaders in the classroom. It is a welcome addition to any library."

Michael Patrick, Ph.D.
Principal Consultant, *M&E Consulting*

"What a valuable resource! Griff Lindell gets to the heart of both leading change and servant-leadership – which the Bible indicates is through a renewed mind and the personal transformation that comes from it (Romans 12:2). *Mastering a Servant-Leader Attitude* contains timely discussion, in-depth research, and penetrating questions that will move you from concept to action. You will want to add this book to your reading list and your library."

Sara Moulton Reger
Business Leader and Management Consultant
Author of *Can Two Rights Make a Wrong? Insights from IBM's Tangible Culture Approach* and *Lead & Succeed: How to Inspire and Influence with Confidence in an Ever-changing Business World*

"*Mastering a Servant-Leader Attitude* will give you 70 Great Questions you can use to Lead Change – first in your own heart and then all around you!"

Bob Tiede
Director of Global Operations Leadership Development for Cru and Creator and Blogger of www.leadingwithquestions.com

"This book is an easy read, but one of the most challenging to implement. From the very first sentence the author writes, you are captivated by the depth of understanding of what it means to be a fully human servant-leader. I dare you to answer the 70 questions for yourself. You will never be the same again if you do! Committed lifelong learners will love this book not only for its intelligence but for the framework it provides for thinking through some of the most important aspects of life. This is one book you won't regret buying and reviewing at every stage of life."

Jonathan Booth
Regional Manager at *LegalShield*, retired CEO of *Care for the Family*, UK (Focus on the Family in the USA)

"Griff Lindell's book is a fresh look at leadership from a Christian point of view. It was the perfect course material to begin my MBA with, and I remember many of the lessons vividly and use the principles found therein with clients and peers alike on a daily basis. *Mastering a Serving-Leader Attitude* outlines the kind of leader I want to be, someone who builds their subordinates up, focusing on their positive achievements to allow them to collectively, as well as individually, reach ever higher peaks of achievement."

James A. Majors
B.S. in Psychology, Future Corban University MBA

"Griff Lindell is amazingly adept at integrating sound leadership theories and practices with Christian theology. His book is a must read for leaders in all industries seeking to approach the workplace with a faith-driven mindset. It is equally noteworthy for students at the genesis of their careers wishing to embrace a faith-filled leadership style. The uniqueness of this book is Griff's comprehensive analysis of leadership theories in concert with an array of self-assessment exercises to help leaders of all types grow. An excellent read and resource book."

Dr. Deborah V. Brazeal
Professor of Entrepreneurship and Innovation

"Remarkable practical! Penetrating lessons born out of the heart on serving-leader attitudes. Expect to be surprise and challenged…brilliant!"

Chuck Ferguson,
Author of *Indomitable Spirit* and *Life Lessons in Leadership*

"Leadership is <u>the</u> defining factor in organizational success. Leading from a biblical, Christ-centered position provides benefits to all stakeholders; namely shareholders, employees, customers and suppliers. Griff has captured and delivered an in-depth look as to what a servant-leader aspires to be and the benefits to all. This book and the questions posed would serve any leader with great insight into themselves and their leadership qualities."

Glenn Duckworth
President, *Industrial Finishes & Systems, Inc.*

Mastering a Serving-Leader Attitude

Transform Yourself by Knowing, Controlling & Giving Yourself in New and Powerful Ways

P Griffith Lindell

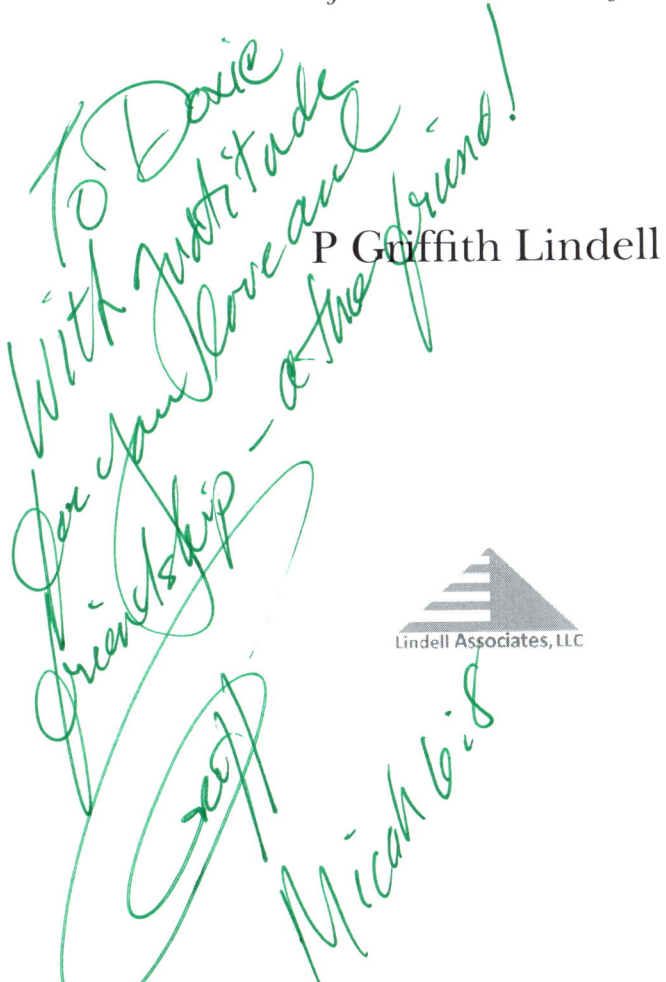

Mastering Serving-leader™ Attitude: Transform Yourself by Knowing, Controlling & Giving Yourself in New and Powerful Ways

Copyright © 2014, P Griffith Lindell

All rights reserved. No part of this book may be reproduced, stored in a retrieval system, or transmitted in any form or by any means – electronic, mechanical photocopy, recording or otherwise – without the prior written permission of the publisher.

This book is a revised edition of graduate-level textbook:
Developing a Serving-Leader Attitude — Knowing Yourself, Controlling Yourself, Giving Yourself: 70 Questions That Will Transform You
Copyright ©2012, P Griffith Lindell

Scriptures marked NIV are taken from the HOLY BIBLE, NEW INTERNATIONAL VERSION® Copyright ©1973, 1978, 1984 by Biblica. Used with permission of Zondervan. All rights reserved worldwide. (www.zondervan.com)
Scriptures marked TLB are taken from *The Living Bible*, Copyright ©1971. Used with permission of Tyndale House Publishers, Inc., Wheaton, Illinois 60189. All rights reserved.
Scriptures marked CEV are taken from the Contemporary English Version® Copyright © 1995 American Bible Society. All rights reserved.
Scriptures marked NLT are taken from HOLY BIBLE. NEW LIVING TRANSLATION. Copyright© 1996, 2004, 2007 by Tyndale House Foundation. Used with permission of Tyndale House Publishers Inc., Carol Stream, Illinois 60188. All rights reserved.
Scriptures marked AMP are taken from the Amplified® Bible, Copyright © 1954, 1958, 1962, 1964, 1965, 1987 by The Lockman Foundation Used by permission." (www.Lockman.org)
Scriptures marked NASB are taken from the New American Standard Bible®, Copyright © 1960, 1962, 1963, 1968, 1971, 1972, 1973, 1975, 1977, 1995 by The Lockman Foundation Used with permission. (www.Lockman.org)
Scriptures marked NKJV are taken from the New King James Version®. Copyright © 1982 by Thomas Nelson, Inc. Used with permission. All rights reserved.
Scriptures marked KJV are taken from the King James Version, Public Domain.
Scriptures marked MSG are taken from *The Message*. Copyright © 1993, 1994, 1995, 1996, 2000, 2001, 2002. Used with permission of NavPress Publishing Group.
Scriptures marked GWT are taken from GOD'S WORD®, © 1995 God's Word to the Nations. Used with permission of Baker Publishing Group.

ISBN-13: 978-1497329768

ISBN-10: 1497329760

Published by:

Printed in the United States of America

Acknowledgements

There are many to thank who spoke into my life in the development of this book, but I want to especially thank Don Coley, Dick Fedchenko, Tim Faley and Paul Lindell (my oldest son). The editing journey for a book can be grueling and thanks goes to David Sanford, Ellen Kersey and Kaitlyn Larson for their individual efforts in finding and fixing my typos, challenging me to write sentences that communicated clearly and also correcting my random punctuation errors.

Thank you to Deb Brazeal, who as a first reader, encouraged me, challenged me to develop more fully some of the leadership styles and then graciously shared some of her academic expertise.

Thanks to Meredith Gould who, at the very start, encouraged me to capture some of my leadership blogs into this book. You inspired me.

A very special thanks to Kent Humphries (now home with the Lord,) who looked at the very first version of this book (in a much different form) and told the truth about that initial direction while supporting my vision for writing about serving and leading. The truth about that first version stung a bit, but transformed my thinking.

To the Corban University MBA students, who use a version of this book as their text for a class in *Biblical Leadership and Ethics*, thank you for finding errors in the manuscript, for challenging me, for pointing out some of my assertions were unclear because I wrote with unstated underlying assumptions and for stating that they could not wait to see the "commercial version" of the book so they could share it with their friends. When I was discouraged with the pace of progress, your encouraging emails and comments spurred me forward.

Thanks Curt Sell for a great cover design and Jessica Marple for working with me to finally get a "good picture" from someone who does not like to pose for photography.

Thank you, Margaret Ann, my dear wife, for laboring with me to transfer the edits to manuscripts and for asking me questions about some of my assertions ("Do you really mean to say *that!*") and for believing in me and supporting me when I wanted to write.

Table of Contents

Acknowledgements vii
Table of Contents ix
A Word from the Author xv
Section I: Getting the Attitude 1
Chapter 1: Why This book? Why Now? 3
    Uncertainty Is the Norm 3
    Servant-Leadership Is a Recognized Model 5
    Do I Have to Believe in God to Believe this Book? 8
    The Changed Heart 9
    People Want Meaningful Relationships 10
    A Serving-Leader Attitude Is a Game-Changer 11
    Followers Yearn for Authentic Leadership 12

Chapter 2: Leadership and Attitude 17
    Leadership 17
    Leadership vs. Management 18
    Leadership Attitude—Not a Leadership Model 18
    No Namby-Pambies Need Apply 18
    Weaving Faith into the Fabric of the Workplace 20
    Principles of the Serving-Leader Attitude 20
    Framework for the Serving-Leader Attitude 21

Section II: Knowing Yourself 25
Chapter 3: Looking Outside Before Looking In 27
    Outside In 27
    Getting Stuff Done 28

Chapter 4: Knowing Yourself by Pursuing Purpose 31
    Introspection—Knowing Yourself 31
    Discovering Personal Purpose 32

Where Are You Headed Ultimately? 34
The Others-Centered Life 35

Chapter 5: Knowing Yourself: Ethics 41
The Battle 41
Training for the Battle 43
Training with Integrity 45
Training in Truth.. 46
Truth in an Ethical Framework 50
Hope in an Ethical Framework 50
Four Attributes for Shaping Ethical Leaders.................... 52
Outcomes for Biblically-Based Leading 54

Chapter 6: Knowing Yourself: Worldview 61
Mental Model—"Seeing" the World 61
Integrating the Past with the Present to
See the Future 61
Worldview and a Box of Chocolates................................. 62
Understanding Worldview 63
Understanding the Power of the Beginning 64
Is It God or Science or Both? 65
Worldview and Teleology... 66
Assessing Worldview 68
A Christian Worldview... 69
Worldview and Commerce... 71
Truth and Worldview... 72
Developing Your Worldview... 72

Section III: Controlling Yourself 77
**Chapter 7: Controlling Yourself: Integration of Body,
Mind & Spirit.. 79**
Discipline... 79
Congruent 80
Defining Body, Mind and Spirit 81
Finding Balance 83
Taking Thoughts Captive—the Mind 84

Avoiding Distractions When Working on Congruency.... 86
Integrating Body, Mind and Spirit 87

Chapter 8: Controlling Yourself: Developing Proficiencies 91
The Learning Proficiency.. 91
The Foresight Proficiency... 93
Foresight—Learning from the Past 93
Dealing with our Fears.. 94
Conceptualizing the Future.. 94
The Clear Communication Proficiency............................... 96
Developing Proficiencies Using an Assessment Tool........ 97

Chapter 9: Controlling Yourself: Behaviors 101
Behave! 101
Why Behave?... 101
Behavior: a Life and Death Decision 104
The Discipline of Taking Our Thoughts Captive 107
Behave for the Joy of It! 108
Healing Others.. 109
Commitment to Personal Change 111

Section IV: Giving Yourself 115
Chapter 10: Giving Yourself: Motivation 117
People Matter 117
Motivating Others 118
You Are Today Because of What You Were Then 119
Praise Will Test a Leader's Motivations............................. 120
Performance Will Test a Leader's Ability to Motivate.... 122
Motivation Is an Attitude, Not a Result of Authority 123

Chapter 11: Giving Yourself: Passion 129
Christian Worldview Motivates Passion............................ 129
A Model for Passion 130
Passion, Practice and Persistence 134
Wholehearted Passionate Leading...................................... 137
Passion's Pitfalls.. 139

Chapter 12: Giving Yourself: Humility 143
    Be Humble! 143
    Know Where To Sit! 145
    Obedience and Humility 147
    Showing Honor 147
    Practice Playing Second Fiddle 148
    Authority and Power 150
    Listening with Humility 151

SECTION V: Major Theories of Leadership 157
Great Man Theory 158
Trait Theory 159
Behavioral Theories 160
    Role Theory Leadership 160
    The Managerial Grid Leaders 160

Participative Leadership 161
    Lewin's Leadership Styles 161
    Likert's Leadership Styles 161

Situational Leadership 162
    Hersey and Blanchard's Situational Leadership 162
    Vroom and Yetton's Normative Model 162
    House's Path-Goal Theory of Leadership 163

Contingency Theories 164
    Fiedler's Least Preferred Co-worker (LPC) Theory 164
    Cognitive Resource Theory 165
    Strategic Contingencies Theory 165

Transactional Leadership 166
    Leader-Member Exchange (LMX) Theory 166

Transformational Leadership 168
    Bass' Transformational Leadership Theory 168
    Burns' Transformational Leadership (TL) Theory 168

7 Transformations of Leadership254 171
Transcendental Leadership Theory 173
Greenleaf—Servant-Leadership 174

Bibliography 175
Scripture Index 181
General Index 185
Endnotes 197
The 70 Questions 209

What does the Lord require of us? It's simple and plain: do what is just, love mercy, live humbly —i.e., don't take yourself seriously. Take God seriously.

Micah 6:8 (author paraphrase)

A Word from the Author

This book is a product of my failures.

And that is the last time I'll declare that judgment about myself, for I no longer believe in *failure,* only in success. In the following pages, I'll write about our constant successes. **We always succeed…in producing a *result*.**

Therefore, this book grew in the womb of the results of my choices—decisions that pleased only me and only for a short time—and gave birth to the choices that did not please God.

The principles I'll introduce were learned in the crucible of my mixed results that did not measure up well to any standard I would be willing to espouse now.

I am a sinner, ashamed of my bad choices, but I am learning from them. I have received God's forgiveness and mercy and moved on. The temptation to dwell on past results remains powerful; however, I'm learning that what the Evil One meant as evil for me, God turned around for His good!

I am learning about the power of God's mercy and grace. I've taken what I am learning and have organized it into a framework to better explain how a sinner saved by grace is now a saint, developing a new attitude about serving and leading as a serious submission to the will of God.

First Timothy 4:7 tells us to "train yourself for godliness." The word we translate as "train" describes young athletes who required training to learn their sport. But their focus was not only the physical training; it also included the idea of mental and moral training. Paul, in this admonition to Timothy, applies it to spiritual training.

This book integrates my learning into my training journey. I have applied the lessons learned into a paradigm for those wishing to lead by applying Biblical (I will capitalize Biblical in the text to always mean the Holy Bible) principles and to develop a *serving-leader attitude.*

Our attitudes shape the results we produce: the question is will we learn from them?

Griff Lindell
Woodburn, Oregon
2014

Section I:
GETTING THE ATTITUDE

"Leadership is a long journey into your soul."

Jeff Immelt

Chapter 1:

Why This book? Why Now?

"If you do not change your direction, you will end up exactly where you are headed."
Chinese Proverb

UNCERTAINTY IS THE NORM

Life is uncertain. Change is a constant. We live in a world pervaded by a sense of instability from the international political scene, to instability of the universe (our sense of it keeps changing—for instance, Pluto is now considered a dwarf planet). For many, the uncertainty of life feeds the gnawing instability of self.

This is certain: effective, authentic, transformational leaders, who have claimed the brand Christian, have learned to develop an *attitude* to lead well when life happens. To make those three adjectives (effective, authentic, transformational) real, I am suggesting that we can learn from those leaders a change in attitude and that one needs to develop a *serving-leader attitude* that is born in the heart, not just in the head. Because it is a *heart* change, its germination is not from human origin, but of Godly seed.

This conceptual framework may trouble some readers. I understand, but would ask this reader to consider two things that interest me: wind and numbers. A strange pair. But related.

Wind—a flow of gases—comes and goes as it pleases. We can describe its strength in terms of breezes, gusts, and more, and those descriptions emerge with our understanding of high pressure and low pressure gradients and the Coriolis Effect. But from where do those pressure gradients come? The wind comes and goes, seemingly at will. We don't really know where it is coming from or where it is going.[1] But we measure it. Feel it. Hear it. Sometimes welcome it. Sometimes fear it. We accept it, but know little about it. We can certainly understand the dynamics surrounding wind, but, conceptually, we just accept wind as a fact of life.

Numbers. Where do they come from? The number five—5—for example is a strange looking number in our writing system. Has "five" always been five or ////? Did "five" evolve from "four?" Or did it just appear?

Numbers are a great mystery. Were numbers in existence before humans? Did we merely discover an existing conceptual framework? If yes, where was that mathematical organization birthed? Certainly, one could not surmise that it was accidental: there is too much elegance in a set of numbers—the style of mathematics, algebra, and calculus is stunning to many mathematicians. And yet, studying the universe through a system of the patterns of managing space, change, quantity and structure of these numbers has provided us with no understanding of which came first: the number or the concept of the number.

So it is with leadership from the heart. I would posit that the fundamental underpinnings of leadership, as a conceptual framework, have existed as constructs since the origins of human life on earth. What I am about to propose for developing a *serving-leader attitude* may not contain all of the possible elements of that attitude, but I suggest that those elements we will develop in this book existed from eternity past, because they were germinated spiritually.

The three pillars of attitude change—Knowing Self, Controlling Self and Giving Self—might, as a set, be considered as the concept of numbers; for I believe that this set of ideas is as useful as numbers in communicating information about relationships. These three fundamental elements of "self" provide us with a convenient organization of attributes to apply effectively when preparing ourselves to work in a community of any kind. The three help us build the kind of attitude that makes a difference in the world. Leader. Follower. It does not matter. To be effective as a leader (with its necessary component of also being a follower), knowing, controlling and giving are foundational to being everything God has created us to be.

Leaders who are developing a *serving-leader attitude* know that uncertainty holds a world of opportunity. However, taking advantage of opportunity depends on the leader's choices and judgments.[2] Although the leadership styles chosen by each of these leaders may differ, for the Christian leader, effective leadership results from an attitude that is others-centered, which is not a natural focus for humans.

That attitude, focused on others, is the rebar in the concrete foundation of life. It is this foundation that will provide stability for handling uncertainty. Life becomes more certain when we know the purpose for it all, and, as Rick Warren famously has said, "It's not about you."[3] Those five words may be the most critical words Warren has ever written about one's purpose for living, and they certainly capture the heart of the person who adopts a *serving-leader attitude*.

Because I'm not a scientist or a mathematician, this book is not about investigating the depths of the "where" and "why" questions of wind and numbers. I'm a simple guy. This is a simple book with a purpose to help the *Christian reader* navigate the waters of uncertainty by developing a *serving-leader attitude* from a Biblical, Christian perspective. Because it is written from a Christian point of view, a simple statement in Scripture captures the essence of *The Serving-Leader Attitude*™ in what is called the *Great* Commandment: "*Love the Lord your God with all your heart, soul, and mind. This is the first and most important commandment. The second most important commandment is like this one. And it is, "Love others as much as you love yourself."*[4]

SERVANT-LEADERSHIP IS A RECOGNIZED MODEL

Although this exploration to follow is not about a model of leadership, in recent years leadership literature[5] has recognized the subject of servant-leadership—some from a secular perspective, several from a Christian perspective. In fact, a body of literature now exists that looks at the conceptual underpinnings of the idea (many based on the work of Greenleaf) in order to develop a theory of servant-leadership. As author R. L. Lengel puts it, "Servant-leadership is leadership upside down."[6] This appeals to me. It is simple, but profound. It is creative and changes my view. It is jarring, but workable. This upside down form of leadership works for me. But it is not the model I'll be exploring. I am writing of behaviors that may be applied to any leadership style you may adopt. As you read on, don't be sucked into the vortex of "ah, another leadership model!" It is not. I'm simply positing that behaviors, grown in the fertile soil of a changed heart, are real now (in our world) and real for the world to come.

However, it is worth noting that servant-leadership, as a leadership paradigm, has been developed[7] describing seven behaviors that often characterize those who adopt a servant-leadership approach. Those attributes are as follows:

1. Conceptualizing
2. Emotional healing
3. Putting followers first
4. Helping followers grow and succeed
5. Behaving ethically
6. Empowering
7. Creating value for the community

Each of these is a great behavior to practice. They have power to change organizations. However, for these behaviors to have any eternal meaning and be truly authentic and transformative, they must be practiced while employing a *serving-leader attitude.*

Remember, this book is not another book on developing a particular type of behavioral leadership style, nor a new authentic leadership model, nor a new form of transformational leadership, including servant-leadership.

This book focuses on how developing the right attitude will deliver authentic *behaviors* from the heart and therefore may be applied to various leadership styles. Section V will acquaint you with many leadership styles and behaviors, as well as personalities and traits associated with many of them.

One must remember that these and other behaviors do not happen in a vacuum, but are influenced by two diverse drivers: the first is the *context* of the leader/follower relationship, and the second is the *natural make-up* (behavioral and personality styles) of the leader. It is this second driver that will be the focus of the early part of the book. Context is developed when discussing controlling and giving of self.

What I have learned, from both my behavioral results that were not honoring to God (sin) and my observations, is that a person who is sold-out to following Jesus has a far better chance of imagining the future, engaging followers, improving outcomes and inspiring their community and, ultimately, society. Imagining, engaging, improving and inspiring are each leadership traits that inform behaviors that are shaped and molded by developing a *serving-leader attitude*.

There may be some fundamental principles here: accept that God is both transcendent and intimate,[8] believe God is holy (a cut above anything else that exists) and understand that God wants a personal relationship with all people (both leaders and followers). Belief in each of God's attributes will yield an authenticity that surpasses trying to follow some set of behavioral guidelines and truths about how humans operate in community without first obtaining a fundamental change of heart.

Authentic (and when I use "authentic," I always mean an authenticity born out of a *serving-leading attitude*) leading begins by following–following well. One cannot be a good leader unless one has *first* been a good follower. A "good follower" is one who has a heart that has been changed from being self-centered to becoming others-centered by following what our Creator has revealed to us. The "others-centeredness" that has meaning, both now and in eternity, results from having a personal relationship with Him.

DO I HAVE TO BELIEVE IN GOD TO BELIEVE THIS BOOK?

Because my network of friends covers a landscape of religious pluralism, I recognize we have differences in our views of God and of faith. To those reading who feel they fit best in a group that does not accept that God has been revealed to humans in His son Jesus (as the only sufficient way to have a relationship with Him), I don't write with a condescending heart nor to belittle anyone's faith—for we *all have faith* in something or someone.

I will accept that many of my underlying assumptions will be difficult for those in this group to accept. I get it. But please remember this book is not aimed to change your beliefs; rather, this book is meant to encourage those who have accepted that Jesus is "the way and the truth and the life…"[9] I want to inspire *you* to consider a bit more deeply what it means to be a leader who expresses a *serving-leader attitude*.

I am reminded of Erasmus, who in 1501 wrote to the "Christians" who "struggled within a world of visible, external formalism,"[10] producing a coldness of religion, not the warmth of relationship. Erasmus wrote:

- *"You observe fasts and abstain from things that do not defile a man, and you do not refrain from obscene speech which defiles both your own and the author's conscience.*
- *The body does not commit adultery, but by your cupidity your mind is adulterous.*
- *You hear the word of God with your bodily ears; listen rather within."*[11]

Erasmus and I are in agreement: the outward signs of religious-sounding lip service and/or good deeds done daily are *dangerous.* Why? Because what God has always cared about, and what matters most, is your *relationship with Him*—a pure heart and a purposeful attitude to do the "will of the Father in Heaven."[12]

THE CHANGED HEART

Truth plays a vital role in changing a heart from a focus on self to a focus on others. Our understanding of the concept of truth is fundamental to our understanding of everything we can possibly apprehend in living. The Apostle John makes it clear that God is not only truth, but he uses a particular word to hone our understanding of what he means by writing "... God is true."[13] What God has said and what He has done are true, because each has been tested and continually proven to be right, pure and true. Pure truth. Evident. Seen. Cannot be hidden or covered up. When it is seen, it is always seen as *true*.

Augustine of Hippo has been paraphrased by Arthur F. Holmes,[14] who wrote that "all truth is God's truth." I would add that since truth belongs to God, truth, no matter its expression, has no meaning separate from God. I would submit that only the Truth of God can change a heart from its natural tendency to serve the self to a new tendency of serving others. However, there are certainly other points of view, other truth providers (Plato, Aristotle, Socrates, Confucius, Seneca, Buddha, Hobbes, Descartes, Kierkegaard, Russell, Sartre, to name only a few) who have developed paths to mold the mind and some even to change the heart, or at least the *karma*.

In the '80's, spirituality began to make a comeback, perhaps to counter the rebellion of the 1960's. Even today, those who declare themselves to be atheists claim to be in touch with their spiritual natures. A modern atheist writer, Paglia, writing in Smithsonian, has noted that "[o]ur new multiculturalism [has] embraced world religions, not as moralistic belief systems but as epic poems convey spiritual truths about the universe."[15] Our views of the arts, science, and life are shaped by what we believe. With the rise of the digital age, many voices sculpt the hard rock of belief systems into images that are too often worshipped in ways that model a devotion Christians should practice when they worship the true, living God.

If any one of these voices shaping the culture's thinking has ever spoken truth, *it is God's truth*. However, although one's insights of truth are God's Truth, it does not necessarily follow that their truths are one of the many paths leading to God. This truth claim of many paths not only contradicts what God says, but also makes no rational sense.

Most religions—all of which claim to work on changing the *heart*—are mutually exclusive in their truth-claims. Buddhists don't believe in a Creator. Muslims believe in a Creator, but don't believe that Jesus died on a cross and rose from the dead. Christians believe both in Creator and a resurrected Savior. They cannot all be true. Christianity, like all "religions," makes truth-claims, and those claims *are* exclusive.

The major difference, that distinguishes Christianity from all other religions, is based on the physical resurrection of a person who claimed Deity and who only asks that you believe and trust in his death and resurrection. This truth-claim is that Jesus's death and resurrection, accomplished on your behalf, is a sufficient means to having a personal relationship with God and producing a changed heart that powers a life that is fulfilling, transformative, and attractive to those are searching for an ultimate, meaningful relationship.

PEOPLE WANT MEANINGFUL RELATIONSHIPS

The changed heart matters, because the question is not what leadership style you use, rather it is what Leader you follow. The "L" in leader is capitalized for a reason: some earthly leaders must be followed for many different reasons, but it is the *spiritual* leader you follow who counts.

Similarly, it is not which religion you choose; rather, it is whose child you are. You can have only one of two parents: either the God of the Universe is your parent (by adoption) or the god of this world remains your parent (by birth). The choice here is a critical, eternal choice. Some are easily deceived, because they hope that humans are all children of God. Scripture does not teach that concept. Jesus makes it clear that to become a child of God one must have an intimate relationship with God Himself. People either worship self (I can choose my own god) or they choose to worship the One who created them in His image.

For the Christian reader, what is the evidence of this choice, this intimate relationship with God? Obedience. Jesus put it simply and directly: "Anyone who doesn't obey me doesn't love me."[16] It is not what we say that matters most. It is not even what we do that matters most. It is who we have chosen to love. The "saying" and the "doing" must then naturally follow. Falling in love with Jesus means we have realized our adoption as children of God and solely believe and trust in that relationship to save us from eternal separation from God. People who choose to fall in love with Jesus know where they are going after this life—being with the love of their spiritual lives—eternally. But those choosing to love themselves and their own ability to make spiritual choices will someday be granted that choice—eternal separation from God.

Don't be deceived: are you in a religion or in a relationship? Religion will never provide unimaginable love that becomes evident in practicing a *serving-leader attitude*. As the Apostle Paul writes, "*I ask Him to strengthen you by his Spirit—not a brute strength but a glorious inner strength—that Christ will live in you as you open the door and invite him in. And I ask him that with both feet planted firmly on love, you'll be able to take in with all followers of Jesus the extravagant dimensions of Christ's love. Reach out and experience the breadth! Test its length! Plumb the depths! Rise to the heights! Live full lives, full in the fullness of God.*"[17]

This relationship with our Creator is critical, stimulated by "what God told us: God has given us eternal life, and this life is in his Son. Whoever has the Son has life, but whoever does not have the Son of God does not have life."[18]

A SERVING-LEADER ATTITUDE IS A GAME-CHANGER

Knowing this—i.e., really believing that Jesus Christ can change our hearts and that this core change is real and certain—is the foundation of developing a *serving-leader attitude*. Without this knowledge, leading by practicing certain "serving behaviors" will not be able to produce a fulfilled, temporal life and a certain eternal life. When leadership gets tough, when the jaws-of-living begin to squeeze your attitude, these behaviors, practiced from the head and not the heart, may disappear. A *serving attitude* must be authentic to whom you *really* are; it must reflect a heart that has been changed.

Behaving as a transformational leader may help those around you, and that is good; but it will not help you have a right relationship with your Creator. That relationship solely depends upon placing your trust in the promise of God that Jesus Christ is not only living again, but is also your sufficient means to God. Your *serving-leader attitude* will then be powered by the Holy Spirit who is at work in your heart and continually transforming you to the image of Christ.

FOLLOWERS YEARN FOR AUTHENTIC LEADERSHIP

Moral leadership, and the character traits that sustain it, can be summed up in one word—authenticity. The authentic leader, starting to live out a *serving-leader attitude,* begins the journey with a guided exploration of self—"knowing yourself." That self-awareness is the result of integrating your understanding of ultimate purpose (your relationship with God) with your ethical framework (how you treat fellow humans) and your worldview (your narrative about life that combines purpose with ethics to understand the past, respond to the present and build for the future).

Christian reader, this process may begin by simply "painting a new picture" of who you are in Christ. The pictures we have in our heads of who we are become powerful. Word pictures that include words like "stupid" or "dumb," "fat," "silly," "slow"—words like this change one's view of the world. The "eyes" of your mind must be pure, clear and positive. Jesus reminds us that *"your eyes are like a window for your body. When they are good, you have all the light you need. But when your eyes are bad, everything is dark. If the light inside you is dark, you surely are in the dark."*[19] You want to be authentic? Control what the eyes-of-your-mind see. People want leaders who are positive, affirmative and open to allowing God to take them places they cannot imagine. Authenticity results from letting go of the fears that haunt you. As fear is diminished, faith may fill the gap left behind. Faith moves one forward to new places that are way beyond an imagination controlled by fear. Authentic leaders, secure in who they are in Jesus Christ, move to a future with eyes brightened from the glory of Christ shining through. This is not manufactured in a motivational seminar; it is made in the still, quiet moments with our God who is in love with us and who wants us to become more and more intimate with Him.

To get to this kind of authenticity, we began by addressing some fundamental questions that focus on origins:

- Were humans created as the result of a supernatural, self-existent, all-powerful being who made matter, energy and time and also made humans in His own image?
- Or are we a "slowly developing" being, the result of random, materialistic processes that, somehow, in a vast amount of time, not only organized the physical substance to make one human, but also produced both mental and spiritual identities?

Your answer shapes your understanding of self and how you go about living an "examined life." C. S. Lewis observed, "There are only two kinds of people in the end: those who say to God, '*Thy* will be done,' and those *to whom God* says, in the end, '*Thy* will be done.'"[20] Said another way, our Creator doesn't force us to love Him. He gives us what we willfully choose to worship—Him or ourselves. Worshipping Him acknowledges that He is the Creator—not some random, naturalistic process that has no meaning and is born simply of start stuff.

For the Christian, the examined life begins, I believe, with the understanding that in the beginning all was perfect. Rebellion to God changed everything then and now changes the way we look at others. It changes the way we look at ourselves. It changes the way we look at culture.

Our culture, and even underlying assumptions in much of the leadership literature, rejects this truth-claim that at one time all was all perfect. This book is based on the narrative that in the very beginning, humans, created in God's image, were fully intelligent, capable and creative, controlling their environment and developing what was needed to live successfully. Life was done well. Serving God. Serving each other. But sin changed that.

Many in our culture (and in generations past) have worked to manage sin (rebellion to God) by denying it and promoting a belief that humans were simply the result of some random, changing process, without a god, without meaning and without an end that matters.

Biblical Truth tells us that humans did not emerge from some animal-like state to the supposed current evolved intelligence. Scripture declares that something radical happened, and humans are moving in the opposite direction from their original created state. Humans are less equipped today to deal with the environment, each other and their own natures than were Adam and Eve.

This truth-claim, I believe, must be foundational to a Christian view of leadership and those adopting a supernaturally-powered *serving-leader attitude*. This attitude emerges from our understanding for *the authority* of Scripture that posits one must believe "*all* Scripture *(*not some, not the ones you want; this is not a menu! All Scripture!) is God-breathed and is useful for teaching, rebuking, correcting and training in righteousness, so that the man [or woman] of God may be thoroughly equipped for every good work."[21]

"Every good work" certainly includes the practice of *authentic and attentive* leadership. That leadership, grown from knowing self, is not an exercise in "self-esteem," but a journey of humility. It must be noted that nowhere in Scripture are we told to seek "self-esteem." Instead, we are warned repeatedly to "not esteem ourselves highly"[22] in relationship to others, whether as leader or follower.

Not everyone believes being authentic is the best path for leading. One psychologist and management consultant argues that "in today's business environment of lean management, shareholder value and fierce competition, authenticity is the best recipe for self-destruction... it is not the quality of authenticity that is required...but the ability to play any role, including the role of the authentic leader."[23] In some mysterious way, this consultant believes that being *authentic* prevents a leader from responding to changing environments and adapting to ambiguity without losing an ethical focus. In the light of the movement away from a Biblical standard to a post-modern view of relativism, this position is an easily understood result. However, this kind of thinking, that moral leadership just cannot work and changing roles is as easy as changing clothes,[24] is destructive and has produced a political environment where the audience, not a core belief system, determines the position to be espoused.

This book's interactive approach is a means to allow God (the Holy Spirit) to speak to you and shape you to become a living example of "Christ in you, the hope of glory."[25] As you work through answering these questions, my prayer is that they yield a moment of clarity about *whose* you are, how you fit in the world, and why it matters now and forever.

May the decisions you make as you answer the questions lead you to finding peace and developing a loving and purposeful *serving-leader attitude.*

After reading this chapter, here are a few decisions for you to consider.

- I'm willing to believe that a sovereign God would not set out to fool us about life's origins; He spoke, and it was.
- I'm willing to consider the implications that spirit, not matter, is eternal.
- I accept that if God can't tell us the truth about our origin, why should we believe Him for anything else?
- I reject your hypothesis about God, or gods, and am going to trust myself to make moral and ethical decisions.
- I want to be in a relationship that is real, meaningful and has eternal consequences.
- I am tired of rebelling and "doing it my way."
- I will trust that Jesus is the sufficient means to God, and, if I die tonight, I want to be with God—His way—by acknowledging that I have been my own god. I want to change that direction in my life and am now trusting that what Jesus did on my behalf gives me a right relationship with my Creator. I'm still not sure how all that happens, but by praying this I believe God will be true to His word and change my heart.

Chapter 2:
Leadership and Attitude

"I don't necessarily have to like my players and associates, but, as the leader, I must love them. Love is loyalty; love is teamwork; love respects the dignity of the individual. This is the strength of any organization."

Vince Lombardi

LEADERSHIP

Leadership has been defined many ways and, at its root, is the concept that a leader has the ability to influence followers toward accomplishing a particular goal or set of goals. A *Serving-Leader Attitude*™ is a process of character development that fits well into many of the current theories. At the outset, I want to make it clear that I hold, as do others, that the "position of…leadership is a division of labor, and in a division of labor, being subordinate does not imply inferiority."[26] Being a leader is not about lordship, but about humility—an attentiveness not only to the vision, but also to those who must willingly and enthusiastically perform to meet the goals that will further the vision.

Leadership does not happen in a vacuum. You must have both a leader and followers, some of whom may be subordinates; others may be peers. Still some may be, in reality, bosses who follow your lead as they grant the authority to lead. Therefore, leadership at its core is a social activity—specifically influencing others toward taking voluntary action. That action, however, is not random. It is purposeful, it has a goal, and it is action with meaning.

LEADERSHIP VS. MANAGEMENT

I look at leadership from the perspective that management and leadership are different. Management is about the tools needed to manage the complexity of an organization; leadership is about leading change. I subscribe to the Kotter model that the tools of management include planning and budgeting, organizing and staffing, and controlling and problem solving.[27]

Leadership, however, is the process of leading the practice of change; it demands the leader establish the direction (vision) for the firm, align people, and motivate and inspire. The latter two influence followers to help move the firm toward fulfilling its purpose and meeting goals all within the set of core values that define how the firm will *be* in the process of both managing and leading.

LEADERSHIP ATTITUDE—NOT A LEADERSHIP MODEL

Again, this book is *not* about a new *model* of leadership; rather, it focuses on a foundational *attitude* that will shape how leaders implement the particular model of leadership they adopt for the situation they are leading. It assumes that many leadership styles might be implemented to achieve the goals of the organization. The many models of leadership (see Section V) provide useful paradigms and can be applied and implemented successfully. The *Serving-Leader Attitude* helps the Christian leader move beyond success to lead with eternity in mind. Work is the place where we most often have the opportunity to live out our faith. People of faith—leading or following—give glory to God when they are effective at work (and at home and play) displaying attitudes that are both effective *and* attractive.

NO NAMBY-PAMBIES NEED APPLY

I have experienced executives expressing something like, "That servant-leadership stuff may be good for you at church, but it's not good for business!" The feeling behind this is that one has to be tough, in-your-face, demeaning even, demanding certainly, to succeed in business. Not so! Those practicing a *serving-leader attitude* may certainly ask tough questions and manage by results, expecting the team to meet expectations. They make consequences known and enforce the results, but always by being firm and fair, not demeaning or dismissive. This attitude is not monolithic. Some practicing the *serving-leader attitude* are analytical—seeking the "who, what, where, when and why." Others may be driven to establish expectations with clearly defined results. Some may truly care about people on the team, but will constantly ask tough questions that demand clear-thinking answers; however, they ask those questions without making those being questioned feel like idiots.

Daft and Lengel quote Bracey (*Managing from the Heart*) about the power—"extraordinary" was the adjective they used—those practicing servant-leadership have over followers and the team. That power—to be sustainable, I believe—must flow from a heart that has been changed by practicing a *serving-leader attitude*. That practice will address five unspoken employee requests:

- Hear and understand me.
- Even if you disagree with me, please don't make me wrong.
- Acknowledge the greatness within me.
- Remember to look for my loving intentions.
- Tell me the truth with compassion.[28]

Tools like these five will raise the bar of your leadership. All leaders must use many different tools to encourage excellence—a goal of transformational leadership. Some tools are meant to train; others, to govern direction and focus; and finally, some provide discipline for inappropriate behavior. Each tool must be used with wisdom and without succumbing to emotional anger or disgust or some other expression of how *we* feel. It should never be about us; it must always be about *them* and helping them succeed.

Coaches often use different tools to train a team. I still remember running laps because of an inadequacy in someone else. The lesson was that we were all in this together. We work together. We are "punished" together. It is about the *team.*

WEAVING FAITH INTO THE FABRIC OF THE WORKPLACE

Motivations to change are both extrinsic and intrinsic—using a combination of each, at the right time, is what effective leaders master. Running a business, at the team level or at the senior management level, demands of the leader clarity about the factors contributing to positive results, the impediments to meeting objectives and what must be done to overcome those barriers. The measure of a Christian leader is how well that leader weaves his or her faith into the fabric of living, both at home and at work.

If we relegate God to Sunday and forget Him Monday to Saturday, we buy into the sacred/secular separation that the lost world espouses. This demand that the two remain unmixed is born of a myth that has no basis in Scripture. One who is developing a *serving-leader attitude* must ask: "Who will I trust and listen to: myth-makers or my Maker?" The position that we must integrate our faith into our work takes strength of character, willingness to risk ridicule for being guided by "antiquated ideas," and the graciousness to realize that those who deny God's role in life are captives. They are prisoners of war, captured by the Enemy of God. The *serving-leader attitude* equips the leader, no matter the leadership style, to be aware that s/he is going into a spiritual battle and must fight, wearing spiritual armor and fighting with spiritual weapons. Suit up!

PRINCIPLES OF THE SERVING-LEADER ATTITUDE

The attitude for becoming an effective leader includes three principles:

1) Being *self-aware* (which fits well into the **Situational Leadership model**);
2) Having the ability to *understand the traits of the team* and adapt the communication and productivity approaches

to best fit those styles (a foundation of the **Contingency Leadership** and **Transactional models** and developed by using the assessment materials recommended later in the book); and,

3) *Transforming one's self first* and then others in such a way that all are passionate about the work they are doing—a tenet of **Transformational Leadership** and the **Servant-Leadership Model.**

These leadership models each have a set of guidelines or observations about ways to behave, to respond to change or to manage complexity, but it is *not* about what we do. Instead, it *is* about what we are becoming. These attitudinal traits are tricky. Without an anchor, our attitudes can be like ships on a stormy sea of emotion, tossed this way and that. The three principles are the strong chains fastened to the anchor, holding a *serving-leader attitude* firm in the stormy seas of leadership. These principles will yield a sense of calm in the blustery ocean of emotions where we must still be about motivating, inspiring and leading others. Leaders want to hold fast since we know that "when the storm has swept by, the wicked are gone, but the righteous stand firm forever."[29]

FRAMEWORK FOR THE SERVING-LEADER ATTITUDE

There are three major foundational principles for the serving-leader attitude described in this book. For each there will be three parts. Think of each "ing" word below as a leg supporting a stool:

1. **Knowing (Socrates**: A life unexamined is not a life worth living.)
2. **Controlling (Aristotle**: Anything in your power to do is in your power not to do.)
3. **Giving (Jesus**: "For even the Son of Man came not to be served but to serve others and to give his life.")[30]

One's attitude to be intentionally pursuing *knowing, controlling* and *giving* can be shaped by considering several verses from the Apostle Peter that provide keys to understanding this attitude transformation:

> We have everything we need to live a life that pleases God. It was all given to us by God's own power, when we learned that he had invited us to share in his wonderful goodness. God made great and marvelous promises, so that his nature would become part of us. Then we could escape our evil desires and the corrupt influences of this world.

> Do your best to improve your faith. You can do this by adding goodness, understanding, self-control, patience, devotion to God, concern for others, and love. If you keep growing in this way, it will show that what you know about our Lord Jesus Christ has made your lives useful and meaningful.[31]

FIRST: Knowing self

Self-assessment is vital to living, and this knowing must be within the context of understanding who Jesus of the New Testament is: *"Jesus asked them, 'But who do you say I am?'"*[32] How an individual answers that question affects how that person examines his or her life.

> *"God made great and marvelous promises, so that his nature would become part of us."*[33]

We begin the process of ***knowing yourself*** by looking at the following:

1. **Understanding Our Purpose**—the essential issues: *"...you may be partakers of the divine nature..."*[34]
2. **Developing Our Ethics**—a framework for how we treat others—our practice of *diligence*. *"...giving all diligence"* includes the thought of *moral excellence*.[35]

3. **Integrating Our Worldview**—a mental model that coalesces purpose and ethics into a narrative of wisdom and knowledge: *"...add to your faith virtue."*[36]

SECOND: Controlling self

Control—discipline—is vital for successful integration into family, work and play. Our key verse comforts us, because it's through His power and our discipline that we can be continually in the process of exercising *control.*

> *"We have everything we need to live a life that pleases God. It was all given to us by God's own power."*[37]

We begin the process of ***controlling yourself***—discipline—by addressing:

1. **Personhood**—congruency between body, mind and spirit: *"peace—which is perfect well-being, all necessary good, all spiritual prosperity, and freedom from fears and agitating passions and moral conflicts."*[38]
2. **Proficiencies**—honing natural skills and developing skills: *"to virtue [add] knowledge."*[39]
3. **Behaviors**—learning triggers and controlling responses: *"to knowledge [add] self-control; to self-control, perseverance."*[40]

THIRD: Giving self

Consciously giving of yourself is vital for developing followers and other leaders. It is not simply a matter of a "rah, rah" attitude or inspirational speeches. It also includes a component of love.

> *"Be completely humble and gentle; be patient, bearing with one another in love."*[41]

The concept "bearing with" is also translated "enduring" or "showing forbearance"—all traits of a person with a *serving-leader attitude*, one who gives self with the others in mind. Finally, we conclude with the process of **giving yourself** by analyzing.

1. **Motivation**—developing the power to influence by serving: "*to perseverance, godliness.*"[42]
2. **Passion**—capturing and sharing motivations for moving in a particular direction: "*to godliness, brotherly kindness.*"[43]
3. **Humility**—assimilating a view that one values others as greater than self: "*and to brotherly kindness, love.*"[44]

This journey reminds me of an old Jewish story about Ben, the shoemaker, who lived a humble existence that provided a simple living. He dies, is about to meet his Maker, and in the "anteroom" bemoans his life, his humble existence, his failure to make much of himself for his family or his business. His lament reminds those in the room of the old prophet Jeremiah in his book of Lamentations. An elder statesman in the room speaks up and warns the shoemaker that when he moves into the presence of God, He will not ask him why he wasn't like Abraham, Isaac, Jacob or Joseph. He will ask you, "Why were you not all that I created Ben the Shoemaker to be?"

This journey you are about to begin is about *you* being all that God created *you* to be.

Section II:
KNOWING YOURSELF

"'Know thy God' (1 Chronicles 28:9) rather than 'Know thyself' is the categorical imperative of the biblical man. There is no self-understanding without God-understanding."

Abraham Joshua Heschel

Chapter 3:
Looking Outside Before Looking In

"A life unexamined is not a life worth living."
—*Socrates*

OUTSIDE IN

The process of self-assessment is inherently difficult. Looking deeply and prayerfully "inside" yields results that will pay eternal dividends. As with many learning experiences we encounter in life that yield positive results, this journey is difficult. The next nine chapters will move you through a period of introspection. A baby's eyes can see, but parents must teach the child to distinguish what is seen (this is red, blue, green, yellow; that is a square, triangle, circle, etc.). Likewise, we have to learn to see the "colors and shapes" of our abilities and attitudes. To help you begin to conceive something new inside you, I have found it helpful to look "outside" first. This change of how you see yourself is not something that happens immediately, but it comes from some hard thinking about how others, with different value drivers (we will consider four), "get stuff done."

There exist two thoughts as bookends to looking outside first. First, knowing *you* is about God and you, *not* peers and you. You were uniquely and wonderfully made: know it, believe it and use it. Second, understanding what it means to be in the process of "knowing yourself" is not about "self-enlightenment." I would go so far to say that it is a concept that is antithetical to today's view of self. It is not becoming a lover of self—satiated with self—which is now encouraged by a society that accepts "me" as a nominative case pronoun ("me and John went to the store...."). This is not a trivial grammatical error—it demonstrates the shift in culture that has permeated our thinking with a self-hyphenated language (self-awareness, self-actualization, etc.)

The great philosophers of the past[45] understood the fundamental nature of this examination of self. Through the centuries, it has been consistently held that all of our interactions with nature, with the spiritual world and with *each other*, begin with a true understanding of self. All that we hope to accomplish as leaders begins with a clear understanding of who we are, by nature, and who we might become by faith. It is our interaction with others that commands our initial attention.

GETTING STUFF DONE

Our interactions are sometimes colored by how we think "stuff" should get done. In fact, that's a common trap: transferring to others our way of leading, promoting ideas, relating and analyzing. Literature has identified these four "styles" by many different titles. The DISC profile uses the terms Dominance, Influence, Steadiness and Conscientiousness. The PACE profile labels are Predicting, Attending, Conducting and Excelling. Smalley/Trent popularized animal types with the names Lion, Otter, Golden Retriever and Beaver. Hippocrates called the four Choleric, Sanguine, Phlegmatic and Melancholic. The Wilson Learning system uses the terms Driver, Expressive, Amiable and Analytical. These systems and others identify behavioral, communication, leadership, sales and social styles. I happen to prefer the Life Orientations Training—the LIFO® methodology—that uses the terms Controlling/Taking, Supporting/Giving, Adapting/Dealing and Conserving/Holding. I recommend the reader discover the styles they prefer the most (and the least) and then determine the styles they use to support their most preferred style may be found online at http://servingleaderattitude.org/LIFO. See QRC code in back of this book.

Before you take this, or any other profile, think about the *first* of this book's seventy questions, which asks you to complete a chart which prompts you to consider four ways all humans are wired. For each, think how those types of individuals accomplish the task listed in the first column.

Write key words—bullet points—(not a narrative) for how you think each type gets something done. I believe this process of looking outside yourself before looking in will help you better assess your leading style.

For example, how do you think a person who is strong on analysis, or driven by data, goes about establishing goals? What are the key words you would use for the style that would be different from someone driven by action when establishing goals?

CHAPTER 3 QUESTIONS

NOTE: a digital version of each of the questions is available at http://www.ServingLeaderAttitude.org using the code SLA-transform. See QRC code in back of this book.

Question 1: How would the following four types of people do each of the following tasks?

    A—Driven by data. Strong on analysis.
    B—Driven by harmony. Strong on concern for "fairness."
    C—Driven by action. Strong on control.
    D—Driven by excellence. Strong on idealism.

TASKS	A	B	C	D
Analyzing				
Exercising control				
Seeking the best				
Sharing vision				
Conceptualizing				
Executing plans				
Providing emotional healing				
Helping				
Empowering Others				
Building community				
Collaborating				
Managing				
Leading				
Promoting ethical values				

Chapter 4:
Knowing Yourself by Pursuing Purpose

"A life unexamined is not a life worth living."
—*Socrates*

INTROSPECTION—KNOWING YOURSELF

Developing the *Serving-Leader Attitude* takes intentional introspection, not some mystical mediation based on emptying the mind and focusing on a sound or body part. Instead, this introspection is focused on your Creator and His purpose for you. Unlike "the Pharisees and the lawyers [who] rejected God's purpose for themselves,"[46] we must know God's purpose for each of us and not ignore it. We have to test ourselves. Look inside. Often. Frank Lazarus, retired President of the University of Dallas, believes that "having a purpose for leaders is of great importance. Purpose requires three things: undying self-discipline, faith, and not allowing a day to go by when you, the leader, neglect or walk away from doing the right thing, whatever this is."[47] The Apostle Paul reminds us: "Test yourselves and find out if you really are true to your faith…"[48] Testing for trueness takes self-discipline, intentionality and a willing behavior that is based on faith in the goodness and mercy of God.

Often we find a gap between our good intentions and our actual behavior. Introspection is a tool to assess our behavior in light of what was intended. Congruent intention and behavior yield a positive impact. In the rush to "get stuff done," effective leaders prioritize their time to find themselves—to examine themselves—learning about what in them helped shape the results they produced. In Lencioni's wonderful leadership fable (*The Four Obsessions of an Extraordinary Executive*), his main character, Rich, frustrated at work and at home, decides to try to eliminate stuff to do at work so he can be with his family. In the process of thinking, he has a breakthrough thought: "Rich decided to turn the nature of his inquiry upside down. He wrote a simple question on a piece of paper: *What is the one thing I do that really matters to the firm?*[49] Introspection can turn your world upside down, especially as you begin to ask yourself the remaining sixty-nine questions in this book. In many cases, the answers may surprise you!

I have found that this examination is often not wonderful, but it is always worthwhile. The time spent in meditation—thinking about what I was thinking about when I did this or that, or said this or that, and then thinking about the response given that did not in any way match my intention—produces an inventory of my actions and attitudes that often need adjustment—the kind of change that offers hope to those I'm leading. The issue is do you want the results you intend or are you willing to just accept unintended consequences?

Poet Robert Burns noted this difficulty of self-awareness while driving the point that we must learn to "see ourselves as others see us."[50] Leaders, especially those claiming to be practicing their leadership style with a *serving-leader attitude*, must develop the ability to withdraw—to see the important distinguished from the urgent and to ask, "How can I better serve those following me?"

We all change. We grow when we learn from the results we produce. That's why this introspection is vital. There is fluidity to life —we must know the direction and speed at which we are moving. Answering this book of questions will help you become aware of the flow of life.

DISCOVERING PERSONAL PURPOSE

Discovering purpose is a not a solo journey: it is finding the *path* God has for you. It's unique to **you** because of what He created in you and the circumstances of life that He allowed for you. How you respond to Him, in love, determines much about your journey.

Discovering your purpose in life is about opening your eyes to the work of His hand in your life. It may well be a new way of seeing for you. It is a journey marked with answers to some important questions. Some of the answers may not be readily apparent. It may take several weeks, even months or years before you discover their meaning, but facing the questions in this book will give you a new grip on living.

Did Cain, Adam's son of Old Testament fame, have a grip on his purpose? If so, he would not have responded as he did to God's instructions. Instead, he would have exercised the control he needed to live out his purpose as a farmer. He ignored God's instructions to Adam and his family; not only that, and unlike Abel, he did not bring the best of what he had—he just brought something he grew. God, knowing his heart, saw the issue: "Sin is crouching at the door, eager to control you. But you must *subdue it and be its master* (italics mine)."[51] That phrase is captured in our word *conquer*—to gain mastery over something, to overcome obstacles.

The path to becoming a leader, especially moving along the path to mastering a *serving-leader attitude*, is paved with stones of truth that are foundational to understanding your purpose. To conquer an awareness of your purpose—*who you are being from the inside out*—you must set the framework of understanding purpose, a framework that includes both what will be written in your obituary and what God might mean when he tells you, "Well done, good and faithful servant…"[52] That way you will be able to "*carefully scrutinize and examine and test [your] own conduct and [your] own work. [You] can then have the personal satisfaction and joy of doing something commendable in itself alone without resorting to boastful comparison with [your] neighbor.*"[53] Your purpose is about you living out what God created you to be.

This takes rigor and a mental "workout" that will yield many results that are vital for two reasons: 1) developing Christ-like character and 2) making real one of the behaviors of the servant-leadership model—providing emotional healing. I have found that rigor is a good word to use, because, as one who had to work to shape a *serving-leader attitude*, I had to work hard to understand my purpose and realize that I often neglected that rigor. Working out your core purpose will help you lead a team, a group, an organization or a ministry. In the Collins and Porras book, *Built to Last*, they note that "Core Purpose is the organization's fundamental reason for being... [It] reflects the importance people attach to the company's work... beyond just making money."[54] What applies to developing an organization's purpose is just as important for the individual. How can you lead effectively if you have not worked out your own core purpose?

WHERE ARE YOU HEADED ULTIMATELY?

The fundamental question is this: how can you lead anyone if you don't really know where you are "going"—both here and now as well as after your death? We spend much time in the leadership arena looking at the *now*. This is important, even critical, to successfully motivating and managing change; however, as a Christian leader, your responsibility extends beyond the *now*. Your behavior and attitude should be so consistent and Christ-like that team-members are driven to wonder "How does he or she do it?" and "What do they know/have that I don't?" In those moments away from the business of running a business, they may ask such questions. The Christian, *pursuing a servant-leader attitude*, must be ready with an eternal answer and not manufacture some meaning from the world's perspective. Then people will see Christ-like behavior in you.

Your answer to such questions will be authentic and attractive only if you have addressed questions about your eternal destiny, i.e., if you know why you are here on earth. You have determined your life, like all lives, is not ultimately an expression of random chance. You are living your unique expression of one who was created for meaning and purpose. You may know someone in your organization or on your team who is struggling, because they believe the adage that *when you're dead, you are just dead.* Others are concerned that choices in this life may have a meaning that has eternal implications, but they have been harmed, hurt, or harangued by "religion" and have used that as an excuse to delay dealing with spiritual issues. "For such a time as this,"[55] God may have put you in that company, on that team, or in that particular group for you to share the good news that you are not shaping a life on your own; you have supernatural help, and it is available to all who ask.

THE OTHERS-CENTERED LIFE

An authentic *serving-leader attitude* builds a life that has meaning; it is not self-centered. Rosoff puts it this way: "In order for your organization and you, the leader, to create a meaningful workplace where people know their work contributes to the organization's success, each one has to know that who they are—as well as what they do—counts."[56] Being *others-centered* is not natural to humans. We are born self-centered, and many of us have continued to live in a state of immaturity, waiting (metaphorically) to have diapers changed and to be fed and burped. To mature, to move outside the *natural,* we must invite the supernatural to perfect us—to mature us. To mature in this manner, we are faced with the choice of believing either that we are just a mass of chemicals resulting from evolution (that somehow produced body, mind and spirit) or that God created humans in His image (*imago dei*) and made them "living spirits"—beings that are eternal. The choice is "goo-man" or "God-man."[57]

Some, who claim the title "Christian" have developed an understanding about God that He is the great "watch-maker" who wound it all up and walked away to let the watch run its course. Others, not willing to take God at His Word, think that evolution really did happen, but God interrupted it (in some mysterious way) to make humans special. For them, whether there was a real Adam and a real Eve is still a matter of debate. For the *serving-leader attitude* to be transformative, I believe that the leader must believe that God's revelation is accurate, that He does exercise sovereign control over His revelation to humans (the Holy Bible), and that He is not playing with us, fooling us, and ultimately deceiving us. His revelation tells us that the Creator God made us in His image, came to us as a human, died for our sin and conquered death for us. He gave us the opportunity to be born one more time, this time in righteousness, commanding us to develop character traits that reflect Christ, to lead by serving, to live by loving—even our enemies—and to persevere in the face of persecutions. These are the foundational elements to an "others-centered" life.

I am contending that those developing this kind of a *serving-leader attitude* believe their chief purpose in life is to "glorify God and enjoy Him forever,"[58] and they have rejected the belief that a personal relationship with God is a religious point of view that is okay for some, but not for everybody. Those grounded with this transforming attitude are not confused by the Zen approach to purpose that holds that humans can conquer fears, find meaning (even in suffering) and choose to be positive in the face of ugly circumstances without a spiritual transformation of the heart from God. While the Zen-like approach may seem beneficial, the question still remains: "So what?" What does it matter if you gain the whole world—conquer fear, display sadness, give yourself to the poor and needy—but lose your soul?[59]

This journey toward developing the *serving-leader attitude* by conquering your own fears and articulating your fundamental beliefs about who you are and why you are here reminds me of a quote by William Penn, who in 1699 wrote, "No man is fit to command another that cannot command himself."[60] To do this you must "make your ear open to wisdom. Turn your heart to understanding."[61] Note the two commands in this proverb—"make open" and "turn." It's a matter of the will demanding a choice. And it's not just any wisdom; it is wisdom that finds its source in God alone.

The leadership stories in both the Old and New Testaments provide foundational understanding about leading. Just knowing about them is not enough, and neither is knowing about the seven behaviors that define the modern version of the servant-leader model. We must turn our hearts (including our heads, hands and habits) toward the God who created us in His image.

What is naturally in us is all about us; what can become supernaturally in us changes our focus to others. That's the key to developing a *serving-leader attitude*. If you want to influence others, first allow yourself to be changed—the head and the heart internally, the hands and the habits externally. The following eleven questions will help in that process.

CHAPTER 4 QUESTIONS

Question 2: Why do you think you are here on earth?

What is your legacy? What will be said about you when your end has come?

Question 3: What should be written in your obituary?

Question 4: What will be your ovation?

When you arrive in Heaven, and your Creator says, "Well done...," what will He list as "talents" you have multiplied for His glory? Consider Matthew 25:19-21, which says, "*After a long absence, the master of those three servants came back and settled up with them. The one given five thousand dollars showed him how he had doubled his investment. His master commended him: 'Good work! You did your job well. From now on be my partner.'*"

Question 5: Why does it matter what you think about?

Question 6: How has your journey of life shaped you in childhood, education, life experiences and relationships?

Look at your childhood, education, life experiences and relationships and consider how these experiences shaped you to date.

Question 7: What is your life vision (or purpose)?

Have you written a personal vision statement? Write a 25 to 30 word statement that articulates your vision.

Question 8: How does your personal vision fit with what you are pursuing today?

Question 9: How will your personal vision drive or shape you in your place of employment or where you might wish to become employed?

Question 10: What mission in life are you currently pursuing?

Think about specific issues you are learning about, working on or pursuing.

Question 11: How does your personal mission fit with what you are doing currently?

How is your personal mission congruent with the mission of the organization(s) where you work?

Question 12: How do you practice self-reflection? How are you learning from the results you have produced?

What is your process for introspection? What are some things you can do to reflect not only an objective camera's view of what happened, but also add the meaning you have attributed to past events? How do you separate the two?

Chapter 5:
Knowing Yourself: Ethics

"A life unexamined is not a life worth living."
—Socrates

THE BATTLE

Imagine visiting an African game preserve. Hot. Sometimes windy. Often oppressive. And yet, in the heat and with a wind that does not provide much relief, your guide still stops your group to point out the wildebeest or gnu. This species of antelope has horns sloping forward, a head that looks very much like an ox, a mane like a horse, and a long tail. These strange looking creatures run in huge herds, creating a tremendous roar as they soar across the African plains.

You may catch a glimpse of a carcass of the Wildebeest lying on the parched African earth, stripped of most of its flesh. Ask any guide, "What happened?" and you will learn that one strayed from the herd and became a lion's meal. The lions are watching carefully, always looking for the one or two that will stray from the pack.

The leader, working on developing a *serving-leader attitude*, faces a "roaring lion" whose aim is to devour anyone who strays. Christians in leadership must recognize that they are in a war! It is a battle of foundational beliefs: a battle for Truth for the individual and the culture. It is a battle of eternal purpose. Our values. Our ethical framework. Many unprepared "Christians" in the business community are losing battles fought in the trenches of practical business decisions. Distracted, dismayed, and discouraged, they have strayed from the herd. They become a meal for the Devourer.

The herd, in our case, may have been our once shared ethical system—sharing made more difficult now by three things: the assimilation of diverse cultures who have *not* become part of the "melting pot" that once defined being "American," the erosion of the family and marriage, and the use and glorification of situational ethics promoted by the entertainment and news media. Each of these present challenges for those who are leading in the workplace. The rules of interaction have changed.

The traditional American value system promotes important concerns—many of which are very good and noble, such as individual health, pollution control, eradication of poverty, etc. However, as Dr. Tim Keller points out, "Sin isn't only doing bad things; it is more fundamentally making good things into ultimate things. Sin is building your life and meaning on anything, even very good things, more than God."[62] Athletes, entertainers and reality TV stars have become the new American idols. Green technologies, Mother Earth or Mother Nature, even creatures like rare birds, butterflies and bugs now are venerated—almost worshipped. We, as a culture, care more about whales than we do about the fruit of the womb. We worship what has been created, crafted or craved more than we do the Creator God. This is an all-too-familiar story. Have we forgotten that idols destroyed the nation of Israel? What one worships can change how one follows or what one expects of his or her leader.

This slippery slope erodes belief in the origins of life by a *Creator*, even if that Creator was the "watch-maker" espoused by those involved in our Declaration of Independence, which states, *"We hold these truths to be self-evident, that all men are created equal, that they are endowed by their Creator with certain unalienable Rights..."*[63] In turn, this denial of our Creator has put ever-increasing pressure on the Christian leader to become shaped by a new pluralistic, postmodern culture that denies an *eternal standard* for our ethics. Keller again points out that "if you center your life and identity on a 'noble cause,' you will divide the world into 'good' and 'bad' and demonize your opponents. Ironically, you will be controlled by your enemies. Without them, you have no purpose... If you center your life and identity on religion and morality, you will, if you are living up to your moral standards, be proud, self-righteous, and cruel. If you don't live up to your moral standards, your guilt will be utterly devastating."[64] I agree! We need to be shaping culture, not being shaped by it.

TRAINING FOR THE BATTLE

The secular leadership community is being shaped by our culture too. A recent study from the IABC found that more than 65% of their membership had no training on ethics, and they advise senior management on ethical decision-making!

It has also been my experience that some leaders who run their business unit, department or company with the application of what we all would call ethical principles, are people who, somewhere in their past, had grounding in biblical truth. Interestingly, many that I have personally known have not rejected Christianity, per se, but it is *religion* in particular they have rejected. The common denominator is that they had experienced religious training in grade school and/or high school, but found the practice of "religion" unsatisfying and not always a positive example of Christ's example of *others-centeredness.*

Today, ethics training that focuses on company values and internal and external relationships is certainly needed; however, the rules, regulations and routes that often flow from that training are generally "head" issues. Heart issues, though, are not generally supported. As Warren Bennis points out, "We are all hungry spirits...motivated to what leads us to find meaning in life... Applied to work, people who feel creative at work are people who contribute to each other and the organization. They seem to find meaning and become meaningful, not lip-syncing other's words."[65] Bennis understands the critical issue: we have to work on the inside first.

Caring and meaning change our focus: how people are treated is certainly an ethical issue. Will Tuttle (Ph.D., composer, musician, author) mused, "Compassion is ethical intelligence..."[66] Understand, I've taken this out of context, for I don't hold to his Buddhist beliefs about animals, diet and world peace; however, those four words are worth considering, because the Christian view of what is called *agape* love can be demonstrated by us when we show compassion to others.

Compassion has deep roots in Christianity, especially in the Old Testament law. Consider: "*When you harvest the crops of your land, do not harvest the grain along the edges of your fields, and do not pick up what the harvesters drop... Do not make your hired workers wait until the next day to receive their pay.*"[67] Compassion is built into God's laws—probably a foreign concept to the secularist and, unfortunately, to many who claim the Christian brand. Behaving ethically is not without its problems—especially since there exists a widespread misunderstanding of compassion as an operating principle. "When one tries to behave in an ethical manner, it is inevitable that he or she will suffer unjustly at the hand of godless people,"[68] warns R. C. Sproul. Scripture reminds us that "when you do good and suffer, if you take it patiently, this is commendable before God."[69] We show compassion to others especially at work, because we understand that it is God for whom we work and God who shows compassion; therefore, so should we.

The discipline of reading God's Word gives us a solid foundation upon which to base compassion *inside* our ethical framework and is also a significant character-builder that will shape developing an ethical framework. Consistent application of compassionate ethics is based on a clear understanding of a human's purpose that is Creator-centered. The foundation of ethics, native to a *serving-leader attitude,* is a heart issue; if the heart is right with God, then the clear application of ethical standards will follow. This paradigm is what will feed our hunger and provide meaning.

TRAINING WITH INTEGRITY

Ethics is often directly associated with integrity. "Leaders can increase their impact by addressing their own morality... To change an organization's values, and ultimately the world, leaders take responsibility for their own level of moral development."[70] At the heart of moral development is integrity. The root meaning of integrity is wholeness—we get our word integer from it—a whole number. Scripture says, "The integrity of the upright will guide them..."[71] The Hebrew meaning of the word used here for "integrity" has in its root the word "completeness" and includes the concepts of ethical straightness and perfection. This ethical framework has strength and integrity. The *servant-leader attitude*, then, is based on "integrity." God told Satan that Job would continue to "hold fast his integrity,"[72] even when his wife said, "Are you still trying to maintain your integrity? Curse God and die."[73] Of course, Job didn't. His ethical framework was securely fastened to his foundation of integrity.

Leaders driven by integrity make a difference. They are the ones who manage change well. Ethical integrity has at its core an obligation of leaders to not only "know self" (as we considered in Chapter Four), but also to establish a personal ethical framework, so they might ultimately develop a coherent mental model—a worldview that makes a positive impact on the people they touch.

One's ethical straightness produces one's integrity. As Greenleaf, the "father" of the servant as a leader movement, pointed out, authenticity—integrity—is at the core of leading as a servant. It "begins with the natural feeling that one wants to serve, to serve first."[74] You understand, this is not a manufactured feeling. It is a natural one (probably better, *supernatural*). Because a Christian has become a "new creation,"[75] that leader now has a real possibility of being authentic, because a changed heart is the beginning of making the crooked straight.

We want our leaders, especially those who claim to be committed to developing a *serving-leader attitude*, to be ethical and speak without dissimulation. We expect clarity—wholeness—

in pointing a direction. That kind of authenticity flows from an "upright" heart, that is a heart in which one's ethics are based on a dynamic relationship with his or her Creator. It is the "heart" of a leader to which people respond. That's why Greenleaf posits that the servant-leader must be "naturally" inclined to serve.

One's job as a leader is to plumb the depths of authenticity not only in one's self, but also by modeling and encouraging followers to do the same. Leaders must ask the kind of questions that connect thoughts, actions and the results produced by team members. Their ethic demands that what they say matches what they do. They are responsible to model and behave with compassion, to listen with understanding and to empathize without accepting inappropriate behaviors or below standard performance.

Just as we cannot create a new primary color, so we cannot change the universal truth (see C. S. Lewis, *Abolition of Man*) that certain things are really true and really false. It is from this ethic that we derive our source of values, which includes respect for the individual. Without that respect, one practicing a *serving-leader attitude* cannot really guide; if one lacks integrity, one will not have committed followers.

TRAINING IN TRUTH

What I am learning is that all of us (a broad generality, I know) need training in truth. There exists a body of research exploring why we humans so naturally lie. Dan Ariely writes, "Everybody has the capacity to be dishonest, and almost everybody cheats—just a little."[76] Christians understand the power of sin nature. What is interesting to me is that the secular world is finding there is a spiritual component to the nature of lying. The research shows that people tend to weigh benefits of lying, even just a little, against a standard. Eight forces seem to consistently drive a little bit of dishonesty, but four forces decrease the urge. Of no effect is the probability of being caught or the amount of money to be gained. What Ariely and his colleagues were looking at were not big issues; small, insignificant cheating issues interested them—and should interest us too. Scripture reminds us that God is looking at how we handle the little opportunities to fudge just a little bit: "*Whoever can be trusted with very little can also be trusted with much, and whoever is dishonest with very little will also be dishonest with much.*"[77] The researchers discovered that "simply being reminded of moral codes has a significant effect on how we view our own behavior."[78] In this particular experiment, they asked half a group to recall the Ten Commandants and the other half to think about 10 books they had read in high school. Recalling the Decalogue had a salutatory effect—in fact, none cheated on the standard mathematical matrix which asks students to find two numbers from a group of 12 that added up to 10 (like 4.81 and 5.19). Swearing on a Bible to do the exercise honestly had a similar effect.

The practice of developing a *serving-leader attitude* and the importance of developing our ethic are both based on God's Word and must drive us to a daily dose of discipline to read and meditate on what God says. If secular research demonstrates that reminders of morality remold a natural inclination to cheat or lie even just a little bit, how much more should believers be committed to capturing the Truth from the One who is the Way, the Truth, and the Life? We have lost much in America by removing the Ten Commandments from our public schools. After all, they have value in controlling behavior, especially if they are brought to mind often. How much more valuable is discovering the eternal laws of God for leading and following. (So, keep reading!)

Those committed to this journey of developing *a serving-leader attitude* have an understanding that both personal moral imperatives (what *is*) and an ethical system (what *ought to be*) must be firmly grounded on a stable, unmoving foundation that finds its bedrock in Scripture. These leaders reflect a personal stability that does not change because of a particular situation. Their stability is based on an unchanging standard, a standard that drives the battle raging in our culture. Truth (with a capital "T") and "The Lie" are at war, and our public schools (and our school boards) are losing. As a society, we have allowed Justice Black's opinion in the landmark case of *Everson vs. Board of Education* to be seen as gospel truth, even though it raised a false barrier between the church and the state by a deliberate misconstruing of a comment by Thomas Jefferson in a letter to the Baptist Association of Danbury, Connecticut. Since then, groups like Americans United for Separation of Church and State have looked for every conceivable way to foster secularism in our culture.[79] Biblical leaders must begin to lead by developing training in Truth in our companies, homes and educational institutions—training to do battle with those who try to dominate the discussion by dismissing standards for Truth.

Truth is a tough issue. The question to consider is if it's true for you, can it be "untrue" for others? Ask secular university students if truth is relative, and they probably will say, "Yes!" Then again, tell them only those wearing the color green will get an "A" in that class, and they then will respond with words like *unfair* or *you can't grade that way*. Yes, they will tell you what "ought to be." In doing this, they show they believe in standards, after all.

Again, can someone's "truth" be someone else's "falsehood"? Hardly. Those who say "everything is relative" are making a "truth" claim. Those attempting to hone their *serving-leader attitude* cannot lead from a framework that includes such self-contradicting proclamations. Yet the culture keeps "taking ground" in this battle, even in the "Christian" community. We have not done well in understanding the ramifications of this war. We have ceded territory needlessly. It's time to stop.

Stopping starts when one considers to whom one looks for wisdom. A leader's source of wisdom determines everything. The Old Testament King Solomon, universally recognized as the wisest person in history, understood Truth as an eternal, fixed standard. The question you must decide is whether or not Truth *really* does have an absolute foundation. If you are not certain, or if you believe that someone's truth may be good for him/her, and if it really does not matter to you what others believe as long as you have a "truth" for you, then you have a very situational and slippery foundation of belief. Leaders espousing such situational principles become open to an ethical system which is morphing to redefine ethics (a standard, *what ought to be*) as morality (*what is*). Our cultural ethic now simply reflects polling—a 51% determination of the will of the people within a given group, culture or system. "Might (of the majority opinion or of the elite-promulgated opinion) makes right." This kind of ethical system makes the practice of developing and living out a *serving-leader attitude* difficult in a world dominated by a post-modern mindset. More importantly, it leads to the destruction of life in the womb, to the recognition of deviant behavior as a protected right, and to changing of the definition of marriage, all of which have impacted the dynamic of the ethical system in the workplace.

Polling to determine what our ethic should be not only redefines the meaning of ethic, but it also destroys any concept of *standards*. This may well be one of the reasons there has been a push to rid public places of artwork displaying the Decalogue. The Ten Commandments *are* a standard. The Ten, however, have been reduced to two (don't murder; don't steal). The other eight have become *The Eight Suggestions for Some, Not All.*

Author David Sanford points out that "indeed, without a divine point of reference, who's to say what's right and wrong?"[80] It is impossible to live without rules. He quotes Ravi Zacharias, who says, "Any antitheist who lives a moral life merely lives *better* than his or her philosophy warrants."[81] I agree with Sanford that we need rules. Humans instinctively know this, and, if they are not following God's standards, they make up their own, hoping that is adequate for living. That kind of thinking, based on "evolving" or culturally "sensitive" rules of moral living, is confusing to both the person creating the set of guidelines and those they influence. Things are changing. All the time. Confusion reigns, especially in the workplace.

Our standard for a business ethic is revealed to us as a Person who demonstrated that He indeed was Emmanuel, God with us. In His humanness, He fulfilled an ethical standard and lived a morally pure life. The Apostle Paul said in Jesus Christ "are hidden all the treasures of wisdom and knowledge"[82] (Truth with the capital "T"). With a close examination of the life of Jesus Christ, the might/right picture has changed. Laurie Beth Jones certainly demonstrated in her book, *Jesus, CEO: Using Ancient Wisdom for Visionary Leadership*, that **wisdom** makes right. That wisdom we are to reflect in our leadership is "not by might or by power but by my Spirit, says the Lord."[83]

An ethical system floating about with a cloudiness of soft edges serves no one—leader or follower. As Gill points out, "Ethical guidelines are just as essential for finding your way in life as good maps and directions are for finding your way geographically."[84] Effective, attractive leadership must be built on an ethical system that honors others and builds an eternal legacy—built on an eternal, solid foundation that does not change with circumstances, court rulings or culture.

TRUTH IN AN ETHICAL FRAMEWORK

Successful businesses with a rock-solid ethical base will serve the needs of their customers in an environment where employees thrive and are rewarded in words and deeds. Employee and customer needs are fulfilled in such a way that the investors' financial needs and the community that physically surrounds the business all profit from the enterprise. Businesses like Chick-fil-A and Toro Service Master, built and operated on Biblical wisdom and based upon Truth, have demonstrated four foundational ethical activities:

- Meeting the needs of other first;
- Honoring and treating them fairly;
- Fulfilling duty (like paying your debts); and
- Showing mercy—Christian love.

HOPE IN AN ETHICAL FRAMEWORK

This kind of foundational framework will enable the person practicing a *serving-leader attitude* to provide a "pure" hope for those following: hope that, in leading change, they will maintain integrity; hope that, in managing complexity, they will show mercy and magnify learning; hope that, in leading people, they will serve others and promote truth. Something that is pure needs nothing added to it; in fact, whatever is added renders it no long pure.

Followers rely on their leaders—especially when a business is struggling—for *real hope*. Therefore, those developing a new attitude about leadership, a *serving-leader attitude*, must be well-centered (knowing their purpose, weaving their behavior into a standard of ethics, and controlling their thoughts and behaviors). As Susan Mallory reports, "Whenever I am in a leadership role, I have felt I have one purpose. This is to help all the people who report to me to be successful. The means my job is to help them define what success is."[85] These kinds of leaders will be able to influence others to follow, because they are well grounded in their ethical system and provide leadership filled with *real hope*. After all, everyone wants to know what success is. In this environment, followers can learn not just how to follow, but also how to lead.

Leaders whose model is the Scripture deliver both hope and an expectation for growth as part of their system of ethics. They are focused on making their team successful. They provide hope, because they see Jesus as the Messiah and fulfiller of their Hope. He still fulfills hope for those practicing a *serving-leader attitude* if they keep their eyes focused on Him, not on themselves or their circumstances.[86]

Modeling this "hope" will happen only if leaders control their self-talk. A Christian's hope is not only in the return of the Messiah, but also in His promise that his Holy Spirit will provide help in daily living. When we produce results we do not like, we need *not* label ourselves as *failures*: *We succeeded in producing a result*. Mistakes happen. Team members may attack you either to your face or behind your back. Your self-talk about these attacks must recognize that God is your shield—your protector. Take this from someone who struggles with self-talk; I have to remember that my hope has meaning and so does my life. Jesus Christ is my hope for a reason. Those adopting this *serving-leader attitude* must not only live in hope. Their lives also must reflect that hope within them—a hope that shapes how they treat others and how they develop their ethical framework.

FOUR ATTRIBUTES FOR SHAPING ETHICAL LEADERS

Business schools demand certain prerequisites for those who want to take advanced classes. Those "fundamental" classes lay the foundation for the deeper thinking required. So also, Biblical leaders have foundational "classes." The 100 level classes help shape an understanding of purpose. The 200 level provide tools to learn to control behaviors. The 300 level teach how to lead from humility. The 400 level integrates all in the daily pursuit of Christ-like character traits. Leaders moving through these classes not only tune into wisdom, but they also apply what they have learned wholeheartedly. They can do this, because a *serving-leader attitude* consists both of reason (thinking) and will (behavior). If the "chief end of man is to glorify God and enjoy Him forever,"[87] leaders adopting a *serving-leader attitude* must start that journey by acknowledging they need to first learn wisdom from their Creator. Then they can begin to build a solid, personal ethical system that will stand in the storms of life.

The result? Effective and godly leaders develop four attributes that continually shape their attitude and leadership by making their "ear[s] attentive to wisdom; inclining [their] heart to understanding."[88] As a result, they "understand righteousness and justice, equity and every good path."[89] This description is worth a bit of exploration.

- **Righteousness**—here meaning conformity to an ethical standard. This word is most often used in reference to judges who, looking at the law (standard), rule without partiality. Leaders have an ethical standard that is absolute and grounded and does not shift depending on the situation.
- **Justice**—here emphasizing the application of the standard, even in a state of ambiguity. Ethics is lived out in

the real world where all things are not black and white. As Hill points out, "...a business act is ethical if it reflects God's holy-just-loving character."[90] Struggling with the "gray of life" is one of the ramifications of eating from the tree of the Knowledge of Good and Evil. It's tough out there. Leaders must exercise discernment, kindness and mercy in morally gray and ambiguous areas. Godly wisdom is demanded—for this discernment must come from a spiritual center. Ego will often cloud judgment—at least that's been my experience. Too often, I have made decisions based on what I thought, not what God thinks. Conforming to the image of Jesus Christ is an everyday commitment of will.

- **Equity**—here used in a clear legal context that means level or straight. The drive to "know ourselves" (wisdom) gives birth to behaving in a way that is "true." There exists, however, a great difficulty here: one can have the best intentions, but it is behavior that makes the impact. A leader developing his or her *serving-leader attitude* cannot be a "straight-shooter" unless his/her heart is plumb, level and straight. That takes lifelong work.

- **Knowing every good path**. "Every." Catch that? Take it from one who has stumbled along and fallen often. "Every" is a tough standard. Interestingly, the word for "good" has a practical meaning—economic benefit. Those practicing a *serving-leader attitude* will find that "a good path" will be presented as an option, but, in the struggle to develop a consistent attitude, it will often be ignored because of the raging spiritual battle. It's that "heart" thing again. One must will to choose the good path. Every time. In his work at Harvard, Christensen urges his students to avoid the "just this once" mentality and live a 100% life—choosing the right path—because it is "easier to hold to your principles 100% of the time than it is to hold to them 98% of the time."[91]

The acquiring of wisdom is a journey, not an event. The journey is not only revealing about "self," but also about the shape and expression of a leader's ethics. Our progress in life is a result of our choices and our willingness to learn from them. Employees and customers often teach the leader about the ethical framework (righteousness) they have used, as opposed to the one they have espoused. Customer service, for one example, is a practical expression about a leader's heart.

Those developing a *serving-leader attitude* must learn to discipline "self" to continue to learn. These leaders work at body, mind and spirit congruence. They actively acquire the skills they need and hone the ones with which they have been endowed by their Creator. They become aware of the patterns of their behavior and the impact such behavior has on others.

OUTCOMES FOR BIBLICALLY-BASED LEADING

Lord Griffiths (Brian Griffiths, former Economic Advisor to British PM Margaret Thatcher), in a lecture at the Peter F. Drucker Graduate Management School at Claremont College in California, suggests that business values—ethics—are based on clear core values. He listed three major values: "Before all else, *respect* for the individual; understand the importance of *truth* in all aspects of business; and a realization that all in the firm are under a set of *binding obligations* that provide consequence when wrong, injustice and undesirable behavior emerge."[92] What is the result for the Biblically-based *serving-leader attitude*? These leaders will behave in a way that expresses love for God (obedience) and demonstrates love for their "neighbors." (Isn't that the essence of *serving* others?) Their leadership will be clothed in justice and righteousness. They will not be driven by greed or personal gain. They will whisper to themselves the prayer of the Psalmist who prayed, "Help me to prefer obedience to making money."[93] Employees will be free to make customer-oriented decisions that benefit the firm. Customers will be attracted to companies that "do business right." Families will be nurtured and grow to love God more and more.

The Biblically-based concept of ethics follows the concepts revealed in the study of the character of God (theology). We act ethically when we reflect the revealed character of God. To be really Christ-like—loving—in a culture that worships tolerance for behaviors that God calls sin and simultaneously practices *in*tolerance for beliefs about what God has revealed as truth, it is all about expressing love and not a judgmental attitude. That love is based on our understanding that those who have not accepted Christ as the sufficient means to God are prisoners-of-war in the spiritual battle for Truth. They are captives. Captives need freedom. A *serving-leader attitude* includes understanding that the leader's behavior reflects God's holiness, justice and love. This kind of attitude-building takes faith that—in the midst of misunderstanding by those captive to The Lie—God still is our refuge, shield, and protector.

Our lives do have meaning. Therefore, our personal and business core values must be clear, consistent and courageous—and yet remain contagious, irresistible and inviting.

Is the ethical framework in your life giving meaning to something that is attractive and pure? The answers to the fifteen questions that follow may help you explore what you really believe and help you find the road to building a solid ethical framework based on how God made you and how well you have responded to Him in love.

As you are working on these next fifteen questions, please remember: "All who are wise follow a road that leads upward to life and away from death."[94]

CHAPTER 5 QUESTIONS

Question 13: When faced with a moral dilemma, what is the basis of the ethical framework you use to address that dilemma?

Question 14: What are the guidelines you use to make choices involving your decisions and behavior?

Do you have an unwritten list that you hold dear and secure? List five to seven words that bring congruency between what you intend and what you do.

Question 15: Do you believe that personal truthfulness, accountability and respect for the individual are without variation even in the face of changing circumstances?

Write about how you might be persuaded to lie a little bit. Think about Biblical examples where personal truthfulness was compromised and yet good was served. Is the latter even possible? Why or why not?

Question 16: What are your core values?

Review what you have written for questions 13 and 14 and find three to five words that would describe your core values. List each and write a sentence or two about them.

Question 17: How do your values impact others?

Think of organizing your thoughts like this.

VALUE	IMPACT ON OTHERS

Question 18: How do you manage moral ambiguities?

Question 19: Describe your source for Truth and why you believe it can guide you?

Is your "source" a rock-solid standard or does it change with the situation? What is the impact of your position on followers?

Question 20: What role does your ethical framework play in your leading?

Question 21: How do your moral choices allow you to help your "team members" define direction?

Question 22: What is the impact of a negative moral choice you might make, and what will you do because of it?

Question 23: What is the role of your obligations? Are they binding or can they be changed?

Question 24: In what ways do your moral choices inspire and motivate?

Question 25: How do you set expectations for those around you so your values are clearly communicated?

Question 26: How do you monitor an inclination to lead from a position of power?

Think of your answer in the context of where you are in life (captain of the team, supervisor, group leader, parent, etc.). What steps do you need to take to begin leading from poverty-of-self (emptying self, allowing the Holy Spirit to fill you)?

Question 27: What are some practical ways to "pay attention" to what God teaches rather than to the shifting ethical framework of the world?

Question 28: How does your life offer hope to a lost world?

Think of a time when you had to stand firmly in your ethical framework: talk about whether "hope" or "helplessness" was an outcome for those involved. What would you change?

Chapter 6:
Knowing Yourself: Worldview

"A life unexamined is not a life worth living."
—*Socrates*

MENTAL MODEL—"SEEING" THE WORLD

The third phase of developing a *serving-leader attitude* will be built on how you view the world: how you see what was, what is, and what you think will be. Developing your worldview demands both reflective understanding and active thinking; however, these activities provide the leader with both temporal and eternal benefits. It is good to remember that "the prudent understand where they are going, but fools deceive themselves."[95]

INTEGRATING THE PAST WITH THE PRESENT TO SEE THE FUTURE

Understanding the past, gaining insights into the present, and contemplating the future seem like a tall order; however, we humans have experience in using past and current experiences to provide the ability to look ahead—to see what might be coming. In fact, many do this often. As a parent or a babysitter, your view of the world of a toddler is far different than the toddler's. Because you have some understanding based upon experience, you look with different eyes at the world than children, who learn by their walk/running legs, exploration, quick movements, insatiable curiosity, and general blindness to potentially harmful events. In fact, in a way, you can see into the future. Therefore, if you are outside with such a child, you hang on tightly to his or her hand. Why? Because the child wants to bolt ahead and chase after things. You know the danger of a small child darting between two parked cars while chasing a cat or bird. The street can be lethal. Your worldview, your mental model, your narrative of what might be demand of you certain behavior. Certain action. A running child, headed for the street, hears a mighty yell, a scream from you meant to scare the child, to make him/her stop. Your worldview has more clarity than the child's. The child's view is sometimes more about the box than the chocolates inside. After all, they haven't tasted chocolates yet.

WORLDVIEW AND A BOX OF CHOCOLATES

Life may just be like a box of "choc-co—lets" (famously said by actor Tom Hanks in the movie *Forrest Gump*); one never knows what one is going to get. Without the ability to read or to have experienced the sweets in that box previously, such a philosophy makes some sense. Many live cautiously, looking for that descriptive label in the lid that tells what each sweet will be. Some boxes provide it. Some don't. The point is that you never get to taste the chocolates until you actually pick one up and start eating. Developing a worldview is like that—it must be diligently worked through to gain the sweetness of the experience. For the Christ-follower, it provides clarity and supports the truth that, in this temporal life, it doesn't matter the kind of chocolate the world delivers. The goodness and grace of God will never follow us with sour chocolate. As children of the King of the Universe, all our "chocolates" are sweet—even in the face of what seem to be ugly circumstances. Think of Job's life. Despite his sour life, he still looked for the sweetness of the God who loved him and showed favor on him. Job's faith was not damaged by what appeared to be a bad box of chocolates. Even when circumstances seem sour, God wants us to give thanks—not thanking Him for the ugliness of life, but thanking Him because He is in control and wants our hearts to trust in His goodness and love. Forrest may well have missed the nuance of looking at the list of the kinds of chocolates, but even a list provides limited meaning if one has never tasted the flavor listed. For many, their view of the world is like a box of candy, never knowing what the sweet will be, but unconcerned "since it really does not matter—at least I have chocolate"—until they happen to get a sour piece!

When people wrestle with a mental model of the world—a worldview—they comes face-to-face with making choices about which chocolates are to be tasted and why they are driven to that choice. The chocolates are all sweet, but each of us has been wired with different taste buds. What you have tasted of the past may drive choices in the present. Sometimes, they may be poor choices, because the meaning you have added to past events is damaging your ability to fully appreciate the present and contemplate the future. Developing your worldview will help you understand the past, the present and your future.

UNDERSTANDING WORLDVIEW

Worldview combines your understanding of purpose and your ethical framework into a model of your ultimate narrative about life—what you believe to be true about life and death—which may be your "box of chocolates." Confusion occurs when there isn't congruence between your views of the past, the present and the future. You are troubled, because life does not make complete sense when, in the dark of night or in the time of trouble, you begin thinking about life and death. It's hard to lead from a perspective that is confused, concerned or not convinced about ultimate issues. It's hard to lead when you are called upon to be willing to *serve* and *lead* at the same time in the same relationship. It might not even make rational sense—like an awful tasting candy. What an oxymoron!

Your worldview is fundamentally shaped by what you think about origins (how it all got started, why you are here, where is *here* and how did *here* get *here*), and it determines what you believe about your coworkers, your family, your boss, and yourself. It also shapes your attitude about leading and following.

UNDERSTANDING THE POWER OF THE BEGINNING

Many books have been written on the subject of origins. This section (as well as Chapter 1) is not an exhaustive treatise on the subject. What one thinks about how we all got here, however, yields certain principles of leading and managing that are often overlooked. We often focus on processes and not on the *purpose* behind why we do what we do—which has it genesis in our view of origins.

Our culture and educational system tell us that "science" has answers for us about origins. God's revelation to humans has been reviled and rejected in our schools, and the new "religion" of scientism now rules. I'm not speaking of the scientific method or analysis of data. Actual science yields many insights that are valid and useful. The religion of scientism or scientific secularism, which has its very own faith positions, is the newest American religion now being taught in the classroom.[96]

Secular religion worshipping at the altar of scientism confuses *cosmology* with *cosmogony*. According to Dr. Johnson, "Cosmology is the empirical (i.e., present observations-based) study of the cosmos as it exists today. Cosmogony, however, is the non-empirical study of how that cosmos began in the unobservable past."[97] The question is, do repeatable scientific experiments help one directly answer questions about the past? I believe the answer is a resounding "No!" because the present is not the key to the past. The past *cannot* be understood correctly by assuming that the processes operating today operated exactly in the same way in the past. Noah's cataclysmic, worldwide flood changed everything. It changed how chronometers may be used to date everything. Despite vast amounts of evidence for a Deluge—in ancient literature, oral traditions, and empirical observations of huge cataclysmic changes in the earth's topography, today's "religion" dismisses the Flood as an ancient myth and as a scientific "impossibility." Impossible? Yes, if one first denies the possibility of God the Creator and Governor of all that is.

The strident voices that vilify Christians in the name of pluralism fail to face the fact that they are promoting a dueling religious perspective. The twin worldviews of humanism and secularism have built their own foundations of faith. They worship materialism, anti-materialism, Mother Nature, the god within, etc. Their faith is based not on revelation, but on the belief that science has destroyed the need for any god—especially the Judeo-Christian God. Their faith tells them that when you are dead, you are dead. Just treat others as you wish to be treated and do no harm (though they have a moving target on what "harm" exactly means).

Often this No-God-Needed view of origins is written and spoken in hidden words. Carl Sagan famously said, "The Cosmos is all that is, or ever was, or ever will be."[98] What is he *really* saying? Do you see? He is saying there is no God. He goes on to say that we are all made of "star stuff." We weren't created; rather, ultimately we are evolved from lifeless chemicals appearing billions and billions of years ago after stars were formed by some massive explosion of energy. Of course, if Sagan had just come out and said, "There is no God," his Cosmos series probably would have been doomed. He was subtle. He created doubt by declaring something as *Truth* when there was no substance of truth in his claim; it was all conjecture, based upon indemonstrable, improvable assumptions. For readers interested in exploring a systematic and Biblical framework for studying the Christian worldview, two resources are of note: a book, *Total Truth* by Pearcey, and the DVD series *The Truth Project* by Tackett produced by Focus on the Family.

IS IT GOD OR SCIENCE OR BOTH?

This atheistic view has gained a foothold in all areas of academic endeavor. When President Calvin Coolidge dedicated the National Academy of Science building in Washington, D.C., he may well not have been aware of the implications of the inscription on that building:

To science, pilot of industry, conqueror of disease, multiplier of the harvest, explorer of the universe, revealer of nature's laws, eternal guide to truth.[99]

So, science is more than just a system of observing and arranging data; it is a system that arranges the data in such a way that "truth" is made available to humans. Certainly, the search for truth seems inconsistent with our modern view of science. Worldviews that reject "nature's laws" and yet yield something "eternal" pose a problem. Such incongruent "faith" certainly impacts how we think about our worldview, our leadership role and our purpose for leading anyone anywhere. A God-assumption, however, not only assumes that His design affects all of nature on Earth, but also everything "out there" in the cosmos and vast reaches of space. As scientists learn more and more about the smallest of things to the largest of things, inherent in each is design; therefore, many predictions can be made about what might be seen based upon mathematical principles. This God, who organized the cosmos to follow "laws" that can be reduced to mathematical formulas, also provides humans with an understanding of behavior—the social sciences—with an organized way of looking at ourselves and others that is consistent, structured and predictable. Our belief in a God who cares to create with meaning and purpose affects our understanding of leading, following and serving.

I see it as simple choice: we either believe that matter is eternal (star stuff) or that Spirit is eternal (God). Either we were created in the image of God, or we are a result of mere goo. Goo- man or God-man. God did not reveal Himself using "goo," of course. Instead, He spoke—and it was.

I believe that a transformative *serving-leader attitude* (one that has eternal impact, not just temporal impact) includes the knowledge that God not only controls what He has created, but also controls the expression of His revelation—the Scriptures.

WORLDVIEW AND TELEOLOGY

Your "teleology," or your belief about the role of purpose in nature, becomes your narrative of how things came to be, what's happened to humans, and what the solution is for the human condition. Of course, secularism rejects teleology, saying nature and the cosmos are purposeless. Life has no meaning. When you're, you're dead. Fundamentally, your teleology will drive your attitude about serving others. If serving others is just a civic duty and an intellectually driven exercise, it ultimately has no meaning. Even if it is born out of religious fervor, unless it is born of God, it has no meaning. Jesus made that clear.

Classical arguments about teleology were explored by many philosophers, including Aristotle and Plato, who saw *purpose* in nature. Today, some writers acknowledge there must be a greater purpose than just what people do in their jobs. This kind of search for meaning is often the foundation of many leadership theories: observation of what people do in certain situations; what that means in that situation; and, based on patterns, what that might tell us about human behavior and interaction.

The expression of the "meaning of it all"—the narrative of existence—was often the subject of classical creative work in music, dance and art. For example, Raphael (Italian painter and architect, 1483-1520[100]) was commissioned by Pope Julius II to produce a fresco to decorate the walls of the Pope's library. To do this, Raphael provided the world with three imposing pieces of art. One of them has been named *The School of Athens* and pays homage to knowledge. In it Raphael used the likeness of Michelangelo as the model for Raphael's visual expression of the great philosopher Heraclitus.[101]

But the central figures of that fresco are interesting, since they express the search for meaning in life. He painted the two great leaders of thought—Plato and Aristotle. Plato's hands are pointing up, indicating his view that it is from the *universals* (the gods) we derive our purpose. Instead, Aristotle has his hand pointing down, for he posited that purpose could be deduced from the *particulars*—the stuff we apprehend with our senses. His view was that what can be seen, touched, heard, felt, and rationally understood are the things from which we can then understand *meaning*.

Our culture today reflects the Aristotelian view. It tells us that what we observe in the present is the key to understanding the past (often called *uniformitarianism*) and that what is seen helps us understand who we are as humans (Sagan's star stuff). Plato, however, was the one on the right track; he just had the wrong deity.

God revealed to his creation the big picture—six days of his Word creating and one day of "resting." One would have to be "willingly ignorant"[102] not to recognize there seems to be purpose everywhere from the microscopic level to the cosmic level. The more science examines what is (data), the more purpose is clearly seen.

From Plutarch's *Lives* to more modern writers, a body of literature has been developed, explaining ways purposeful leaders must think and behave to motivate followers. Each writer offered valid ideas and processes on leadership. Studies have emerged from many disparate disciplines that have shaped and augmented this literature. Each writer—some intentionally, many without intention—has reflected a particular worldview, a view about "nature's" purpose.

ASSESSING WORLDVIEW

Nancy Pearcey, writing in *Total Truth*, developed a three-part model to help form our understanding of worldviews. Each worldview…

- Assumes something about origins (fundamentally either matter or spirit—first cause—is eternal);
- Defines the problems that beset human beings (at the core it's either sin or some evolved set of environmental/societal drivers); and finally,
- Ultimately offers a solution to the human condition (either redemption through the work of God, in Jesus Christ, or some form of societal, sexual or governmental solution).

Our view of these three attributes determines our views about the intent, behavior and impact humans have on each other and the role that leaders and followers play in that dance of interaction.

God tells us that effective leaders are first followers of Him. These followers then lead by example; therefore, effective leadership begins after a heart is changed from its original nature to a Christ-centered nature. A heart changed will shape behavior toward yourself and others.

Man's theories come and go. God's laws have remained constant. How we view ourselves (our very "origin," our view of Truth, our role in society) impacts how we view others (their value, importance and meaning). Leaders are people who are centered and therefore can love others in a way that builds community—a team—with honest, encouraging camaraderie. The first governor of Massachusetts Bay Colony, John Winthrop, gave these words to his fellow colonists in 1630: "We must delight in each other, make others' conditions our own, rejoice together, mourn together, labor and suffer together, always having before our eyes…our community."[103] Leaders invest the time to develop the habits needed to apply the heart and tune the ears so that, with true altruism, they can give themselves and build a real, authentic business community.

Leadership that promotes followers and builds new leaders is framed within the context of serving and giving. Authentic leaders—who give time, resources, insights, instruction, encouragement, and energy—are demonstrating by their actions that they are developing the kind of attitude, if from the heart, that will please God. All these attributions are developed and honed within the context of a teleology that believes this life has eternal meaning and that one's worldview is critical to better distinguish The Truth from The Lie and the impact of each on a *serving-leader's attitude*.

A CHRISTIAN WORLDVIEW

We have been deceived! We are told over and over that the secular world and the sacred must not be mixed. In our secular society, a Christian worldview has become equal to a Buddhist, Hindu, or Muslim worldview. They may have different "truths," of course, but those "truths" are simply details people can ignore as they practice anything, including leadership. The normative narrative is stated something like this:

- "What might be right for you does not mean it is right for me."
- "Keep your values to yourself—glad you have them, but I'll find my own."
- "What make you think your worldview is right?"
- "Religious views have no place at the public table."
- "Our constitution says there must be a separation between church and state."

As Pearcey suggests, in our culture (and this definitely applies to the literature of leadership) a line is drawn between what she calls the "upper story" and the "lower story." This provides us with a picture of the two *worlds* where matters of faith and value systems are in "the *world* of the upper story," and matters of fact, science and public policy are in "the *world* of the lower story." The secular view is that the two worlds are separate and not interrelated and therefore:

- What you do on Sunday (if you go to church) must *not* be brought to work on Monday;
- God is good for some, may be okay for you, but is not for all; and
- God is just a "manufactured" god;[104] therefore, God is treated as "common and ordinary,"[105] driving a pluralistic, secular worldview.

It is becoming increasingly evident that a new standard is emerging that holds that the Christian integrated worldview (where there is no boundary line between what is sacred and secular) is "hateful," because it dares espouse standards. These standards are seen as "personal values" that belong in the upper story and therefore cannot intrude on the thoughts, ideas, attitudes and behaviors in the lower story. Some of the pluralists and secularists among us (including some in the public media) hold that this intermingling is not just hateful, but also harmful and haughty (arrogant). Our culture has created a spirit of "fear" for those who want to hold up a divine Standard: we can be demonized, marginalized, ridiculed and rejected.

Those of us who integrate our faith into our work must reject that "fear," for fear controls what you believe to be true, and that belief will control you. The person working on his/her *serving-leader attitude* remembers that "God has not given us a spirit of fear and timidity, but of power, love, and self-discipline."[106] And, in *that* spirit, those incorporating a *serving-leader attitude* will lead with standards clothed in love and mercy. Those willing to adopt this *attitude* must lead by applying Christ-like behaviors *not from* their core of "getting stuff done" that separates work, from play, from home, from faith, *but from* an integrated core that maintains that one is the same in each instance, expressing a different focus, but not a different person.

WORLDVIEW AND COMMERCE

A Christian worldview recognizes that God is the source for maintaining truth and justice in affairs of commerce. "A just balance and scales are the Lord's; all the weights of the bag are His work [established on His eternal principles]."[107] A secularist sees the weights and scale as simply man's evolved ability—man's ingenuity. The philosophical two-story worldview in which we live (faith, feelings, etc. are in the private, upper story; science, math, commerce, etc. are in the public, lower story) is blind not only to the source of the materials upon which creativity is applied, but it also denies the Source of all. The Creator God, who became man, forever broke that false barrier. It is He—our Creator—who put the concepts of "just scales" in man's heart, so that no man can alter them without violating God's rights and authority. "God cares about honesty in the workplace; your business is his business."[108] The righteous leader knows God is all and in all—even in work.

Christian leaders live in authenticity by adopting this worldview that fully integrates God's revelation and man's knowledge of life. It defines what it means to walk in the "way of understanding."[109] That walk includes (1) unifying our public/private, sacred/secular lives and (2) gaining spiritual power.

TRUTH AND WORLDVIEW

The Christian perspective is that Truth is not subject to man's rules about discourse and debate. Understanding the principles of *Truth* is vital since many business decisions are not clearly legal or illegal; rather, they often demand leaders to think about which paths should be followed—and that takes understanding, a clear focus on the Truth and a firm grip on one's ethics. Sometimes we cannot clearly see down the path; following God's lead is a walk of faith and not sight.

This faith walk begins with "knowing God," and that results from feasting at the table of His Word, filling time with scriptural prayer and fulfilling the mandate to have transparent relationships with godly people. These three—mentors, meditation, and memorization—are character-building attributes that will help develop your worldview.

DEVELOPING YOUR WORLDVIEW

The development begins with thinking about some foundational questions:

- Why are humans on earth? How did we get here? Have you thought this through in a way that will help you motivate, inspire and challenge followers? In the beginning, we assume something about origins (fundamentally either matter or spirit—first cause—is eternal).
- What is the human condition? Are we just blank slates imprinted by environment and DNA? Are all humans sinners? We define the problems that beset the human being (at the core it's either sin or some evolved set of environmental/societal drivers).
- What is the answer—the solution—to the human condition? Is our salvation a good education? Riches? Government? The Lord Jesus Christ?

The book of Job reveals that God cares about our worldview. Job apparently wrestled well with these questions. Even in the midst of horrific circumstances, he knew who he was, what guided him and how that fit into his worldview. He was an authentic leader.

This is your opportunity to think through your mental model of the world (the integration of purpose with ethical principles). Use the following nine questions as a screen to understand the past, interpret the present and anticipate the future. Developing your worldview will help you manage ambiguity in Christ-honoring ways at each turn now and in the future.

CHAPTER 6 QUESTIONS

Question 29: What is your creation narrative?

Write out your beliefs about creation. Was it in six days or six eons? What are your conclusions about importance?

Question 30: What do you believe is the problem with humans—the human condition?

What is your belief about what has happened to the human race? What is the human condition? What is responsible for that condition?

Question 31: How is the human condition solved? What is the "redemptive force" that will change the human condition?

Question 32: What is your worldview?

Synthesize your responses to questions 29-31 into a worldview. Attempt to sum up a clear personal statement of faith that reflects your worldview.

Question 33: How does your worldview motivate you to live out your core values at home, at work and at play?

What do you believe to be true about human behavior and its relation to living out one's core values?

Question 34: In what ways does your view of the world reflect or reject the current culture? Implications?

Question 35: How do you anticipate problems and use your worldview to help ameliorate them?

Question 36: After considering your worldview, how does this change your purpose statement?

Question 37: After considering your worldview, how does this change your ethical framework and your core values?

Section III:

CONTROLLING YOURSELF

"The cyclone derives its powers from a calm center. So does a person."

Norman Vincent Peale

Chapter 7:
Controlling Yourself: Integration of Body, Mind & Spirit

"What is in your power to do, it is in your power to not do."

Aristotle

DISCIPLINE

Control of our emotions, thoughts, speech and behaviors is an inside-out process. King David of Old Testament fame was called "a man after God's own heart,"[110] because, despite his humanity, he was committed to building from the inside out. His predecessor, Saul, initially shy and apparently humble, did not work on his heart, and his hubris got the best of him.

Controlling self is an integrated function that begins with an understanding of what controls humans. Leadership literature increasingly recognizes the importance of the body and mind (and spirit) being in balance. When leaders discount one for the others, however, problems arise. Work-life balance has become an expected corporate policy with the focus mainly on resting the body and giving the mind something different on which to focus. They miss the point: body, mind AND spirit must be congruent and in harmony to exercise self-control.

CONGRUENT

Congruent is defined as:

1. Agreeing; accordant; congruous.
2. Mathematics—of or pertaining to two numbers related by a congruence.
3. Geometry—coinciding at all points when superimposed: congruent triangles. [111]

The geometry definition paints a great picture: triangles are congruent if two pairs of corresponding angles and a pair of opposite sides are equal in both triangles.

Congruent triangles are exactly the same whether rotated or mirror (reflected) images of each other. In the figure on the left, both triangles both have two corresponding sides equal in length and with the same angles. As a result, both are congruent, even though one is a rotated mirror image of the other.[112]

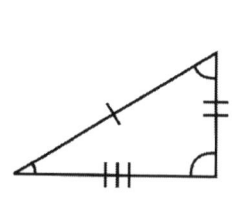

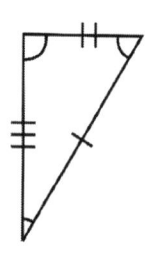

When you add a third triangle—each one representing one of the three attributes of body, mind and spirit—all three must be congruent, which raises some important questions.

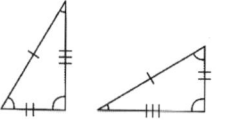

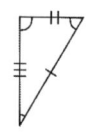

Body: Do you keep your body "in shape" so your life and work are not affected by excess?

Mind: Are you developing the habits to become a lifelong learner?

Spirit: Do you respect the individual, reward integrity and seek the will of God?

Charles Dickens made a good living exposing businesses that worked people too many hours to the detriment of their bodies. We have work-rules today that recognize that humans need to rest their physical structures. Dickens also exposed those who focused on the mind to the exclusion of the spirit. These characters lived as if the body and mind were all that is—and the spiritual component of humans was dismissed as not important—indeed irrelevant. His writing, as well as others since, has given rise to a leadership perspective that became increasingly more sensitive to the complete person. Today, leaders must recognize all three natures and manage business accordingly.

DEFINING BODY, MIND AND SPIRIT

It is my belief that humans are both material and immaterial beings. Some writers in the area of theology posit that humans are two-part beings, consisting of body (material) and soul (immaterial). Others distinguish the immaterial into two distinct, but interrelated "parts." I hold to the second view.

Body—material. "*The Lord God formed man of the dust of the ground.*"[113] This is the temporary housing for the mind and spirit. When humans die, the body dies—returns to "dust." Its chemical nature breaks down and becomes part of the ground from which it was originally created. The body has sensory-consciousness, which can be used to the destruction of humans: "*And when the woman saw that the tree was good (suitable, pleasant) for food and that it was delightful to look at... she took some and ate it.*"[114] Thus, sin began its journey into the world through Eve's sensory gates.

Mind—includes your beliefs, attitudes, feelings, emotions, memory, will, thinking, reasoning and desires. Like the body, the mind must be controlled. "*And when the woman saw that the tree was...to be desired in order to make one wise, she took of its fruit and ate.*"[115] As Aristotle noted, "What is in your power to do, it is in power to not do." The mind and spirit are mysteriously connected at the seat of your self-consciousness and, if left to dominate, can destroy your eternal relationship with your Creator. The word "soul" is sometimes used to represent the human consciousness—awareness and response to stimuli.

Spirit—the part of you that is the essence of life. "*...and breathed into his nostrils the breath of life; and man become a living soul...*"[116] It is the "you-ness" of you—what makes you an individual, distinct from another. As above, soul is often used to mean spirit—or one's life essence.

Your spirit is the power that ignites you and controls you. When theologians tell us that humans are born in sin, they are talking about this spirit that is born evil and must be supernaturally reborn to become good. Your spirit is either of God or of sin and this gives meaning to life and helps you define your purpose (which can be changed when the spirit is changed). From your spirit you form your faith, your communication with your Creator (prayer) and your ability to have God-consciousness. It is this within us that can be regenerated so we can know God and the things of God, for "*...the natural man does not receive the things of the Spirit of God, for they are foolishness to him: nor can he know them, because they are spiritually discerned.*"[117]

When humans were created, it is this spirit that ultimately distinguished humans from the animals. "*Then God said, 'Let us make man in our image, in our likeness...' So God created man in His own image, in the image of God He created them; male and female He created them.*"[118] The Apostle John reminds us that God is not material, and we share an attribute of His, for He made us in His image. "*God is Spirit...*"[119] It is from our spirit that we worship either ourselves (we choose our own god) or our Creator God.

FINDING BALANCE

We now seem to be living in the *body* generation—we worship the body. Movies, entertainment and sports are each about the body—the material you. It may be a bit of an overgeneralization, but it could be argued that the Reformation worshiped the *spirit*; the educated opinion-makers of that time focused on things spiritual. In the same manner, thinkers during the Renaissance worshipped the *mind* and reasoning; what the human soul conceived was venerated, and God was not.

Those who want to make real a *serving-leader attitude* should keep the three in balance and worship the Creator, not any one part of the creation: "[Those who have rejected God as He has revealed Himself to us] *exchanged the truth of God for a lie, and worshiped and served created things rather than the Creator—who is forever praised. Amen.*"[120] Being out of balance is a sign we are worshipping something other than Jesus—it may even be good deeds we are doing for the church, for our family and/or for others. Jesus was balanced. He refreshed His body. He grew His mind. He nourished His spirit. Even in the midst of His intensive three-year ministry, He took time to be alone with God. Balance is difficult, especially for those of us who have goals to meet, people to mentor, programs to develop, and processes to be implemented. We often are driven to look for the return on our investment of time, because we are about implementing our strategy, fulfilling our vision, meeting the benchmarks for our mission, and monitoring how we and the team are "present"—show up—in the pursuit of our goals. Values matter, but monitoring and managing them take time. Leaders are often known for "getting stuff done" and in the doing often move, well, too fast. In his book, *Ordering Your Private World*, Gordon MacDonald[121] tells a story that illustrates this point in a memorable way. A traveler was making a long journey into the jungles of Africa and, having hired locals to carry the loads, made incredible progress the first couple days. Hopes were high, from those who hired the natives, that this would be a speedy journey. However, the third morning, the native tribesmen refused to move. The traveler, getting a little frustrated, pressed for a reason and was told that the natives, quoting an old African proverb, said they had gone too fast and were now waiting for their souls to catch up with their bodies.

Sometimes we need to slow down—at least I know that has been true for me when I have pressed forward to meet business goals. My life, far too quickly, got out of balance. Keeping these three in balance is not merely an intellectual pursuit, as much of the leadership literature would have us believe. The secular world wants to strip God out of the process—except for the spiritual—and allow you to choose whatever "rings your bell." For the Christian, seeking earnestly to live in balance by controlling our behavior—what we think about and how we "see" life—it would be good to remember something Pearcey points out: "The path to intellectual renewal is to offer up one's entire self—mind, body, heart, and spirit—in solidarity with the sacrifice of Christ. Anything less can become pride and empty intellectualism."[122] The world has enough emptiness. Those developing the *serving-leader attitude* do not need to add its emptiness. As leaders and members of the Church (universal), we "must seek to conquer not merely *every* man for Christ, but also the *whole* of man."[123] Those pursuing a *serving-leader attitude* practice T.A.G.—time alone with God. We must pursue God if we are going to lead others. We must pursue God, not the doctrine *about* God. God. As Jesus pointed out in the Sermon on the Mount, pursuing God is a hallmark of those taking the narrow path. But, if we lose our balance and our focus, even walking the narrow way can become about *us*, instead of God. Our doctrine may be correct, but it is not our doctrine that nourishes us, that balances us. Instead, it is our trust that a loving Savior is yoked to us to pace us, to lead us, to give us the power to do His will and His work.

TAKING THOUGHTS CAPTIVE—THE MIND

What you learn and study is important; so is what you think about, because how one thinks fuels behavior. Dwelling on what others think of us is not healthy. When a person looks only externally for behavioral anchors and makes decisions congruent with those external behaviors, trouble may occur. This book presents a process to get in touch with internal anchors that will provide you with a "backbone of steel" in the face of potential ridicule, derision or simple misunderstanding. Your mind will be engaged as you thoughtfully address the answers to the questions following this chapter. They will help develop a spirit of wholeness; they will show you that doing things right speaks to your body, your mind and your spirit.

I once made a decision to accept a position with a firm about which I had some lingering doubts. The office shown to me—high above the shores of the Pacific, where I could see miles of curving coast line, and miles of ocean—seduced me, and I said "Yes!" to the offer to join the business. As I sat in what was to become my new office (a big, bold and beautiful room), I started getting sick. By the time I arrived home to talk to my wife, my body was screaming "NO!" I was sweating, my mind was racing, my stomach hurt and my spirit definitely was not at peace. Fortunately, my wife brought to my attention that my body was talking to me and that I'd better listen. I did. Calling up the CEO, I told him that my body, my mind and my spirit were telling me in no uncertain terms that my "Yes" must become a "No." I turned down the position before the contracts were typed and sent for a signature. I learned that to become a centered leader, I must be continually developing a *serving-leader attitude* by using internal anchors. I was learning to listen to my body to control behavior.

I had let my thoughts run wild looking out that window, even though I knew that I was to "*throw off* [my] *old sinful nature and* [my] *former way of life, which is corrupted by lust and deception. Instead,* [I was to] *let the Spirit renew* [my] *thoughts and attitudes.*"[124] We choose what we want to think about: it is a matter of exercising our will and being intentionally attuned to the Spirit's leading. This is a matter of exercising great discipline, and my story illustrates how easy it is to slip—allowing a big office with a killer view to slay what in my Spirit was wrong for me. I willed to deny it, but God was gracious—He allowed my body to speak to me and my wife to gently point out that I was not listening.

The Apostle Paul warns, "Set your minds on things above, not on earthly things."[125] How is that accomplished? The Apostle provides a path to a solution by telling us that we are not only to teach that principle to others, but also personally practice taking "captive every thought to make it obedient to Christ."[126]

Taking thoughts captive requires "spiritual jujitsu." Use the energy of your thoughts to springboard into thanksgiving to God who provided you with a creative imagination. Because the Evil One does not want to be around when you are praising the Almighty One, replace ungodly thinking with what "is true, pure, right, holy, friendly, and proper. [In fact,] don't ever stop thinking about what is truly worthwhile and worthy of praise."[127]

This thought control produces peace that beams from you like a searchlight from a lighthouse at night. Done in a spirit of humility, you light up the environment so brightly that all around see and wonder exactly what is the source of that steady light of apparent peace. Peace follows when you are committed to an integration of how you are viewing and treating your body, how you are developing your mind and how you are nurturing your spirit.

You demonstrate by your life, by your actions and especially by your words that "the spirit" (heart—emotional intelligence) is the fuel for the engine of the mind and body, for "what comes out of the mouth gets its start in the heart."[128]

AVOIDING DISTRACTIONS WHEN WORKING ON CONGRUENCY

Perhaps an office overlooking a beach will not distract you, as it did me. Whatever may grab your attention, as a leader, you are on a journey to develop the "soft side" of leadership by developing sensitivity to the qualitative aspects and character issues. The Scriptures say: *"Dear [reader] listen well ... Concentrate! Learn it by heart! Those who discover [Biblical words of wisdom] live, really live; body and soul, they're bursting with health. [Also, they] keep vigilant watch over [their] heart; that's where life starts. Don't talk out of both sides of your mouth; avoid careless banter, white lies, and gossip."*[129]

If you are in management, for example, are you expecting your sales team to produce revenue to the exclusion of integrity, using white lies, exaggerations, manipulations, and under-handed dealings? Authentic leaders have learned to lead change well. They must develop a process to reward both the positive results produced by followers *and* the constructive character traits expressed by those followers. Rewarding both produces the best long-term results.

How do you go about nourishing your body, your mind and your spirit? Do you allow your team to actually take *real* vacations—or are they on call 24/7? Not only is that probably a violation of the law, but, more importantly, it is a violation of God's law that rest is *good* and important for His creation. Just as you do not take a drink of water only one day a week, neither can you nourish your mind and spirit for two hours on a Sunday morning. You nourish your body by drinking liquid every day. How are you treating your spirit and your mind? (The Biblical term "heart" is a unique combination of both.)

What about your mind? Does what you are learning now, built on what you have learned in the past, end the learning process? What is the latest leadership book you have read— and studied (meditated upon)—for self-learning, as opposed to formal learning? How are you nourishing your mind with more than technical data about your products/services, the industry or the marketplace? Do art, music, fiction, poetry, gardening, hiking and other creative pursuits provide nourishment for your mind and spirit?

The "heart" fuels the engine of your mind and body. How do you practice reflection to keep your heart pure? Your motives pure? When you look at the results you have produced at work, home or play, how do you reflect upon them to change behavior in a way that will produce different results? What is your experience with apologizing—recognizing that the results you just produced did not honor God or other people?

INTEGRATING BODY, MIND AND SPIRIT

The image I use to illustrate the body/soul/spirit integration is the Statue of Liberty. Like many illustrations, it is not perfect, but it is useful. The statue is an integration of the flame of the spirit, the crown of the mind and the structure of a supporting body. The foundation for this symbol is both large and solid.

Another illustration from Scripture might be instructive: Noah's three sons named in Scripture are Ham (body-physical), Shem (spiritual) and Japheth (mind-intellectual)—each may represent regions and nations that mirror the tri-part makeup of humans.

The *serving-leader attitude* is based on a balanced integration of body, mind and spirit for the purpose of learning more about what our Creator has made in and for us. We are reminded in Proverbs, "It is senseless to pay tuition to educate a fool, since he has no heart for learning."[130] The heart changed by God will allow the learner to absorb knowledge, understand truth, and respond to authority in ways that a purely secular approach will never achieve. As Johannes Kepler is credited with saying, the study of science and the universe is a process of "thinking God's thoughts after Him."

Faith that the Jesus difference is a distinction of vital importance drives the reality of His Spirit living within us to provide the power needed for self-control. On our own, our attempts for control are temporary, and, under stress, that self-foundation becomes obvious. Only a supernatural "Rock of Ages"—the Messiah promised to the world—the living Jesus Christ provides the foundation we need to exercise control.

Is your life built on the shifting sands of self or the living Rock of the Ages? Integration of body, mind and spirit takes work. Do you have a work plan? The questions that follow this chapter are asked to help you keep your life in balance. They will require work that must be clocked in prayer, which demands much of your mind. They may force you to meditate on a process of integrating your body, mind and spirit in a way that will reflect how you are wired and how you want to continue to grow. As you complete these four questions, allow the Spirit of God to be the fuel in the engine of your work.

CHAPTER 7 QUESTIONS

Question 38: Analyze your day: how much time do you spend on your body, your mind and your spirit?

What are you learning?

Question 39: How do you make the connections between your body, mind and spirit stronger?

How have you been intentional about nourishing all three? Do you work 12 to 14 hours a day? Do you work seven days a week? Do you skip vacations ("I don't have time")? How does that schedule help or hinder nourishing your body, mind and spirit?

Question 40: What process are you developing to "take every thought captive"?

Question 41: Do you journal? If not, what process do you use to learn about the results you produce at work, at home and at play?

Chapter 8:
Controlling Yourself: Developing Proficiencies

"What is in your power to do, it is in your power to not do."

Aristotle

THE LEARNING PROFICIENCY

Life-long learning is an attribute of leadership—especially of those seeking to hone their skills as leaders committed to living out the *serving-leader attitude*. "*A wise man will hear and increase in learning, and a man of understanding will acquire wise counsel...*"[131] Note the parallel construction in this proverb. The word *counsel* is used only in Proverbs and Job and means to guide and direct with the attributes of right thinking and experience in decision making. Its construction reflects an increase in learning. We are to acquire counsel, which speaks of a life-long learning process.

Throughout recorded history, wisdom has been institutionalized, and with good reason. The wise were about sharing, training and producing wise people. We learn from history. We learn from the imbued wisdom of intact teams who have been with an organization for years. We learn from the learned. Even Plato's understanding of what people thought about and developed was based on his research of ancient writings and oral traditions passed down from the generations of Ham,

Shem and Japheth. Humans have been continually in the process of learning from the time humans were created.

Leaders must continually be learning *how* to be all they can be—better understood, learning *how* to be all God created them to be. As one learns, one changes, and those changes produce more change. Do those leaders practicing a *serving-leader attitude* need to have certain personalities with a particular set of attributes? Thankfully, no!

Drucker, in his classic article "What Makes an Effective Executive,"[132] observed that those leaders with whom he had worked had a panoply of personality types, values and personal strengths and weaknesses. What he did discover was eight practices for which effective leaders developed proficiency. "The first two in the following list gave them the knowledge they needed. The next four helped them convert this knowledge into effective action. The last two ensured that the whole organization felt responsible and accountable."[133]

- They asked, "What needs to be done?"
- They asked, "What is right for the enterprise?"
- They developed action plans.
- They took responsibility for decisions.
- They were focused on opportunities rather than problems.
- They ran productive meetings.
- They thought and said "we" rather than "I."

These eight become alive when the leader not only develops (hones) his natural, positive behavioral and personality traits, but also works to develop and enhance less used skill preferences. It is this discipline of development that helps the leader better grasp the knowledge needed, turn that "knowing" into meaningful action and motivate followers to manage both personal and professional change in mutually beneficial ways. That kind of leadership sees something that others may not.

THE FORESIGHT PROFICIENCY

The power of foresight allows leaders to see opportunity even in a world of issues and problems to be solved. Leadership foresight—an attribute of Greenleaf's *The Servant as the Leader* thinking—is the result of the synergy between the **lessons of the past** and the **realities of the present**. These are connected in such a way that the potentials for both intended and unintended consequences in the future represent the right thinking at the right time and in the right manner. So, how does one develop foresight? How does a leader plot a course?

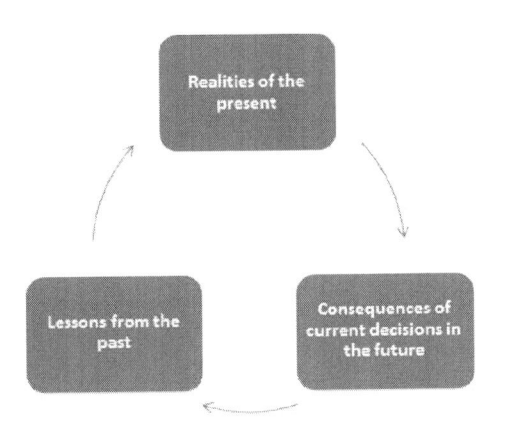

```
         Realities of the
            present
        ↗              ↘
                        ↓
  Lessons from the   Consequences of
      past           current decisions in
        ↖              the future
           ←
```

FORESIGHT—LEARNING FROM THE PAST

Plotting a course begins with learning from the lessons of what *has* been done. Journaling is a great tool to help facilitate that learning. As you read your journal, you will gain insight into how you chose to look at what happened in the past. Many use the past to define the present, clinging often to a harmful or destructive past to provide a narrative for today. Effective leaders have learned to move out of judging the past into a mindset that looks for lessons that will help shape accepting of the reality of today without coating it with the patina of the past. It is not only difficult to live *today* by looking in the rear-view mirror, but it is also nearly impossible to see the opportunity of the future if the eyes of the mind are continually being shaped by a negative focus of what has been and the resulting self-talk about "what happened"—and our associated but mostly unspoken fears.

DEALING WITH OUR FEARS

Rolling Stone magazine famously asked, "Is it *perception* or *reality?*" How we look at the present is often shaded by our perception of our fears about what happened in the past. Fear is all around us. It's real. It always seems to try to control our thinking. Conquering fear is a proficiency that takes discipline to develop. Laurie Beth Jones[134] tells the story about an exercise she uses to teach a group of female physicians how to conquer fear. One was chosen to be the "heroine" of the story in the Kingdom of Fear [my words, not hers], and her job was to take an object—let's call it the "magic ring" [my words, not hers]— and put it in a cup across the room. Others are chosen to be the heroine's worst fears. The rules were that those playing "Fear" could not physically touch the heroine, but they could do almost anything else. They moved chairs to block her view, shouted, screamed and hollered—anything to distract her from her goal. But she persevered—as you and I must do.

Your present reality might be plastered with real fear, and how you handle it will shape your future. Follow the example of The Servant-Leader, Jesus. Jones points out that "Jesus knew that the best way to conquer fear was to face forward. He did not shrink from going to Jerusalem. He boldly announced his identity to his executioners. He got sick to his stomach and wept till sweat became blood—but he went through it. Although he felt fear, he faced it."[135]

CONCEPTUALIZING THE FUTURE

Actions have consequences. One mode of foresight provides leaders with an understanding of not only intended consequences, but also discernment for unintended consequences. The latter is a result of asking good questions that reflect an understanding of what happened in the past and the lessons learned, as well as a keen awareness of what is going on in the present that is not being shaped by fear.

This ability to conceptualize is a prime talent of successful leaders. They know how to dream great dreams that have an anchor in reality but a focus on the future. They know how to think beyond the day-to-day of getting stuff done, and they constantly nurture in others the ability to see and live in the completed future. These leaders operate like an artist who gives the world great sculptures by developing the foresight to look at a huge chunk of marble or granite and see a finished form, therefore removing only what is necessary so the finished sculpture appears. Developing a *serving-leader attitude* will help you gain the perspective of the artist who works at getting rid of anything that interferes with the revelation of the completed future.

Let's slightly modify the metaphor: a *serving-leader attitude* drives the kind of ability that artists possess to outline the completed picture in charcoal and then paint the scene with colors that express the artist's creative expression. Those committed to living out a *serving-leader attitude* differ in one major respect: they do not paint the picture alone. They "see" the finished picture, share their passion for their vision of the completed future of that picture, and then they allow their team—who have different skill sets, different drivers of what is of value and different ways of communicating—to paint the picture. Done well, this seemingly impossible task of taking the diverse "colors" of the individual team members will produce a beautiful result—a completed picture—of what was first envisioned. Todd Siler in his book, *Think Like a Genius,* quotes a nineteenth-century German chemist Justus von Liebig, who wrote, "The secret of all those who make discoveries is that they regard nothing as impossible."[136] Those who practice leadership foresight are driven by the same relentless spirit to allow the team to help paint the picture. In the practice of leadership, it is not about the "artist" leader. It is about the collaboration of the team that completes the picture—a task that demands of the leader discovery of what each member of the team can provide to complete the "picture" of a task, a mission or an initiative of the enterprise.

THE CLEAR COMMUNICATION PROFICIENCY

Corporate culture thrives when clear communication is a core value. So do family cultures. Thriving occurs when the leaders *and* the followers are committed to become more and more proficient in creating clear communication. This is best expressed when each person at every level of an organization (a team, a family, a group, a firm) embraces and accepts as legitimate each of the values of a personality style (values like harmony, action, excellence, reason, etc.). Leaders who practice a *serving-leader attitude* must develop the kind of culture that supports communication without fear, including challenging the way "things are done." Clear communication cultivates the kind of company that "speaks" with integrity, because its employees do. Leaders must recognize that even idle words can be dangerous, and what a leader says does matter. Effective leadership in this positive culture is about keeping the "air clear."

How easily communication can become polluted. Believers are admonished that our words must make a difference: "The tongue of the wise uses knowledge rightly, but the mouth of fools pours forth foolishness."[137] We are called to be purveyors of peace with words that are fitting to our listeners—words that encourage, edify and empower.

The stored-up knowledge and experience of team members and leaders becomes most useful when communicated wisely. It takes care to communicate "rightly"—proper time, proper place and proper thoughts. I understand this so very well, because sometimes I fail to wisely communicate. I blurt out—what a foolish thing to do.

Using any of the many personality inventories gives clues to how people process information—and how to speak their language. Hershey/Blanchard's Situational Leadership posits that the right leadership communication style is based on the person being led: leaders communicate with awareness so relationships can be built. That's using knowledge rightly. Foolish people practice "throwing it out there to see what sticks," with no concern to the listeners' style, their underlying fears, or where they are in life experience. That's more like "belch[ing] out foolishness"[138] than speaking.

DEVELOPING PROFICIENCIES USING AN ASSESSMENT TOOL

The book includes links to the Life Orientations® survey, which I greatly encourage the reader to experience. There is a charge for taking the online version of the survey and receiving a personalized report based on your results.

The survey measures a person's relative preference for four basic behavioral styles. These styles are not competencies, so participants are not labeled, judged, or limited by their survey results. As I have written earlier, labels are dangerous; that's why I do not believe in *success* or *failure* as labels. Actions produce results. We learn from results. Labeling someone with a personality type can become an excuse for sub-standard performance ("I'm no good at that—I'm just not that type of person") and an excuse not to learn, not to keep honing the skills with which you were born, and not to work at tapping into your little-used, but existing, skills and traits.

The report is *your* report, and it is based solely on how you answered the survey questions. It will give you a good understanding of the skills, behaviors, values and beliefs that you prefer, both when things are going well for you and when you are operating under stress.

You also will learn why people behave the way they do and how to use that information to best communicate with individuals to motivate understanding and positive action. In other words, you will learn how to communicate in your listener's communication style—not *your* style. Maybe even more importantly, you'll learn that there is no one right way to "do stuff."

As you may recall, Question #1 was asked to prepare you to develop a *serving-leader attitude* that's committed to understanding. After completing the Life Orientations survey, you will be well served if you go back to Question #1 and reflect on what changes you might make from those in your original response.

To take the survey, go to http://servingleaderattitude.org/LIFO. See QRC code in back of this book.

The following two questions will become richer, deeper and more instructive when you include what you are learning by taking the survey and assimilating the observations included in your personalized report.

CHAPTER 8 QUESTIONS

Question 42: What is the most recent non-fiction book(s) you have read or are reading? What have you learned that applies to learning to manage or lead?

Question 43: What is your plan to be a life-long learner?

How will you learn to apply your strengths well, moderate their excesses, and develop a versatile approach to communication?

Chapter 9:
Controlling Yourself: Behaviors

"What is in your power to do, it is in your power to not do."

Aristotle

BEHAVE!

Hopefully, by now you are committed to developing a strong degree of self-awareness. You want to understand the impact of *your* behavior on others—as well as the impact of *their* behaviors on you. An attitude focused on the needs of others will drive you to moderate your strengths when needed, capitalize on them when appropriate, and supplement them when necessary. You will develop the discipline to increase awareness of your behavior and its impact on others.

WHY BEHAVE?

Your behavior can dominate even a benign situation. I learned, the hard way, that my intentions were not always in sync with my behavior. In one instance, as a manager, I was using my familiar behavioral interactions—honed as a teacher of junior-high students—that were very unrealistic (to say the least!) for the team I was leading in a technology company. I needed to learn how to behave in a way that was appropriate for the environment I was in by changing my behavior to match my intentions. Learning this takes intentionality.

You can role-play responses to certain stimuli, and that does create a meaningful skill set of reactions. What it does not do, however, is prepare you for reactions that cannot be predicted or that you just cannot even fathom ahead of time. Parenting is a good picture of what I mean. Babies—who cannot verbalize except by crying and sometimes smiling—can elicit in adults reactions that are beyond rational understanding. The frustration of not understanding the crying baby, when the crying does not stop, often leads to inexplicable feelings in adults. Before babies can speak, they seem to have developed some ability to "push buttons" in their parents that parents did not know existed. These behaviors are an expression of deep-rooted beliefs that have yet to be addressed by the adult parent.

In addition, driving a vehicle often generates behaviors that seem to come out of nowhere. Drivers sometimes make emotional choices that, for the most part, are not woven into the fabric of their relational spheres of life. Inside the car, some behaviors emerge that one might never exhibit around people with whom one must interact.

Why behave, anyway? The ancients wrestled with this question. Lao Tsu[139] reminded people that behaving is an act of surrender: "Surrender yourself humbly; then you can be trusted to care for all things. Love the world as your own self; then you can truly care for all things."[140] Bad behavior finds its source in self-centeredness, not in others-centeredness. Focusing only on one's self blinds people to the consequences of their behavior and its impact on others. The Golden Rule is forgotten, because the focus is on themselves and the impression they want to make on you. Consequences to self-centered behavior are often unintended, because people don't take the time or energy to contemplate consequences. They act and let the chips fall where they may. A *serving-leader attitude* is built on the realization that a leader's behavior matters. So, one must practice self-discipline to stay focused on controlling one's behavior to the benefit of others.

That discipline of one's self demands of the believer a spiritual commitment that includes meditating on God's Word, prayer, and an awareness of the need to moderate our strengths when under stress. I have found that constructive criticism is sometimes hard on the ego. I know the person offering advice means well—I just don't hear it well. The wise thinker wrote in Proverbs, "*If you listen to constructive criticism, you will be at home among the wise. If you reject discipline, you only harm yourself; but if you listen to correction, you grow in understanding.*"[141] This listening takes discipline, a willingness to be open to learning, and a commitment to grow. If you build around you a team, willing to help each other grow, the result is a certain freedom to listen, respond, change and grow. Sometimes, though, the situations that bring the "worst" out of you are not clear, moral choices. Instead, they are ambiguous.

In his seminal work *Good to Great,* Jim Collins observed that freedom and responsibility may result when leaders build a *culture* with people who "take disciplined action" and are "willing to go to extreme lengths to fulfill their responsibilities."[142] Fulfilling responsibilities sometimes presents moral dilemmas. How you behave as you manage moral ambiguities is first determined by how well you have wrestled with knowing who you are and your personal purpose. Alexander Hill reminds us that "Christianity does provide guiding principles; it does not for the most part provide detailed technical rules of conduct. Rather [it] focuses on the spirit of the law. It recognizes that gray areas exist in which there may be reasonable disagreement."[143] Controlling behavior requires a clear understanding of one's worldview and its impact on the people being led. Look to our model—Jesus Christ—who certainly pursued holiness perfectly while showing a measure of tolerance toward those who did not measure up to His standards of behavior. When He supposedly "lost control" in driving out the merchants from the Temple, He did *not* actually lose control. He exercised restraint, but clearly demonstrated that the behavior of the money changers was unacceptable, given the purpose of the temple and the exercise of true faith. Sometimes, one has to take a stand.

I am concerned that many students coming out of public schools believe that morality is nothing more than an expression of a cultural understanding of the greatest good for the greatest number. They have been taught that positive behavior is a result of a march in humanity's evolution and that behavior is often a factor of the lack of nurture. Forgotten is the Biblical story that the behavior of ancient humans became so bad that God destroyed that world and began again with Noah and his family. Instead, students today have been told that man created God, not the other way around. Ignored is the evidence in archaeology, oral traditions and ancient texts that early societal groups were so vile and evil that they were destroyed. Some of these stories became the fables that generated the Grecian tales of gods and goddesses. What is interesting is that these tales have equivalents in the traditions of many American Indian cultures, as well as many Central and South American traditions.[144]

The concept of being born in sin is foreign to current thinking, which espouses that humans are born *tabula rasa*—as a blank slate onto which behaviors are imprinted, shaped by the environment. The government's role is to address poverty, which has grown as a result of a capitalist focus that forgets people in the pursuit of profit. Yet is behavior just a matter of culture and its mores?

Perhaps the answer may be found in the role death plays in our behavior. If when you die you remain simply dead, then behavior must be the result of a positive evolutionary process. However, if there is a judgment after death, i.e., if there is "life" after death, then there may be other drivers for learning how to best control our behavior.

BEHAVIOR: A LIFE AND DEATH DECISION

The question of life after death has produced much discussion among philosophers and religious writers. Plato—no doubt influenced by Socrates' teaching—used analogy to argue there must be life after death. What he saw was a cycle common in nature: winter leads to spring; day follows night; seeds die before flowering; the butterfly emerges from a rather grotesque caterpillar, in an ugly cocoon, after a period of dormancy (the "death" of the caterpillar). However, as nice as these analogies are, they are not compelling evidence.

Another thinker, Immanuel Kant, noted that all humans have some concern for ethics, and, although the moralities may differ, they all wrestle with behaviors—what is right and what is wrong. His observation led him to ask questions. Perhaps those questions could be summed up by asking: "What would be necessary for this human sense of the duty to behave to make sense?" Kant realized that for ethics and a culture's morality to be meaningful, there must be justice. So he asked the question: "Why be ethical if justice does not prevail?"[145]

R. C. Sproul[146] deals with these issues of why we behave by explaining Kant and providing a framework that's helpful for this discussion. Based on Kant's question, for there to be justice *after* death, based on how one lived *before* death, someone has to receive the justice. Justice does not exist in a vacuum; it exists for people. After all, we can all agree that many don't get justice here on earth during their lifetime, so they must be able to get it after they die. If they do not, ethics is not practical, and behavior does not really matter.

If there is justice, there must be a just judge, and justice requires that judge to deliver a judgment. But for justice to operate justly, the judge must be utterly and completely just. This judge cannot make mistakes. Sadly, in this life "just" judges *can* make mistakes—no one is perfect here. However, perfect justice in the next life demands a perfect judge. This logical thinking was all very practical for Kant. It is worth noting that Kant was not building an argument for the existence of God. Instead, he was trying to deal with the ethical issues of controlling behavior, and his conclusion was that humans must live *as if there were a God.*

How much better it is to live *knowing* God. *As-if living* does not demand discipline. Since it's only *as-if living*, then if one's behavior does not live up to a certain standard, it really does not matter, because *as-if living* presupposes there is no end that matters. For the Christ-followers, however, understanding behavior begins with knowing God, since the discipline to control ourselves, operating from our own resources, is folly. Then again, for a personal relationship with our Creator to have any meaning, that relationship must provide the tools we need to behave. Christianity tells us that on our own we are lost, ultimately lonely, and captives both of our sin nature and of the evil ruler of this present age. It tells us that those "captives" may do many good things and operate as ethical and good people—some may even be committed religious people.

A personal relationship with Jesus Christ is *the* tool box holding various tools needed for living a life pleasing to God. The good news is He supplies the tools and stands there with the tool box in His hands ready to hand it to all who simply ask for it. Inside are tools for knowing yourself and controlling yourself and giving yourself. Our problem is that we are so used to trying to do each in our own power that we don't often take advantage of the means God has given us to live a life pleasing to Him.

Controlling self is a critical stage in learning how to lead with a *serving-attitude*. This stage requires discipline that reflects your determination to change your approaches and responses to behavior yielding different results. This proverb makes it plain: "*Whoever loves instruction and correction loves knowledge, but he who hates reproof is like a brute beast, stupid and indiscriminating.*"[147] To put the proverb quoted above more simply, "to learn, you must have discipline."[148] I'm reminded of what Scott Peck said in his book *The Road Less Traveled,* "Without discipline we can solve nothing."[149] To grow personally as a leader demands you not only practice self-discipline, but also learn from the "discipline" of others. Both have the power to shape your work and your life, so you can better pursue the direction needed to create positive change.

But note also what these words of wisdom tell us. We are not to tolerate discipline, not just deal with it, not simply accept it, but *love it.* Those practicing a *serving-leader attitude* learn that the results from every action taken provide a learning experience. They see the decisions made, the behaviors practiced and the actions taken *as producing results.* These leaders have learned not to pronounce judgment on the results in terms of success or failure. The *key* to learning to love discipline—the *attitude of loving* discipline—is to *learn from the results you produce.* If you don't like the results, change what you are doing. Don't be a "brute beast, stupid and indiscriminating." Learn. Change. Grow. Live this life knowing that the next life matters. What you do *here* produces results *there.*

THE DISCIPLINE OF TAKING OUR THOUGHTS CAPTIVE

Giving voice to thought is sometimes easy, but often words are just blurted out. I do understand, for I have learned that putting my tongue in gear before my mind is engaged is dangerous. The habit is difficult to control. Those practicing a *serving-leader attitude* must learn to take captive their thoughts.

But there is a more critical, fundamental issue. It is not just about controlling what we actually verbalize; it is controlling what we think about. As the Apostle Paul noted, "We take captive every *thought* to make it obedient to Christ."[150] What one chooses to put into the mind matters. His or her thoughts must be taken captive—for a purpose. Why? Because out of the mouth flow the intents of the heart.[151] The one follows the other, especially with the problem of greed. Our greediness is generally our own—it stays in our mind, or so we hope. Greed, however, is an attitude that finds its source in wanting something someone else has and scheming to get it. I think the root of greed is covetousness—the breaking of the tenth commandment—the great hidden sin. This may drive our self-talk in ways that will eventually harm us in our interactions with others. We can be greedy for many things: power, prestige, acceptance, money, influence—or other "stuff"—including a corner office. Jesus reminded His followers and us by warning, "Beware! Guard against every kind of greed. Life is not measured by how much you own."[152] Controlling greed is not about manipulating God (if I control my greed, He'll give me the desires of my heart); it is about obeying him. Contentment is a great antidote for greed and Scripture reminds us that "godliness with contentment is great gain."[153]

BEHAVE FOR THE JOY OF IT!

Controlling both our thoughts and our voices takes intentionality—in other words, *control*. Those adopting a *serving-leader attitude* develop ways to control both thoughts and talk, and the result of that control is joy. Joy is a powerful force. When I first started teaching high school back in the late 1960s, my master teacher clued me in: she told me that if I created clear boundaries for the students and demanded they control their behavior (including their body language) then I would have a joyful classroom where learning would thrive. I was struck by the word "joy," but later learned she was right. The students knew who was in control, and they also knew there were immediate consequences for their lack of control, whether speaking when others were, or talking without permission during lectures, or writing and passing notes in class (which, if caught, I'd read aloud—if appropriate—sometimes I had to monitor the language!) or just plain day-dreaming in a way that distracted. They felt *free* within the boundaries I set, and therefore I soon could have them sitting in groups, not rows, working as teams on homework and learning to collaborate and learn from each other.

Control yields joy for both the person and the people with whom the person interacts. Because one disciplines the mind to be filled with both the knowledge of God and what one has learned from all the results produced, being able to give a right answer can yield joy. Building up, not tearing down, people yields joy. Encouraging others is joyful. Providing advice when asked brings joy. Saying the right thing at the right moment is a joyful emotion for the speaker. I learned these principles in the classroom and then in business. It wasn't until later in life that I noticed that all along God's word was teaching the same principle: the fruit of our words should be sweet and tasty—delightful to the ear. Scripture tells us that "a man has joy in making an apt answer, and a word spoken at the right moment—how good it is!"[154]

Remember, words we say provide only a small portion of communication. The larger portion consists of what our body's posture speaks and the tone of voice we use. I am learning that sometimes I still struggle with tonality or being harsh when I'm interrupted or have been concentrating on something else. I have learned that taking captive my tone of voice is a process of character-building—continually being conformed to the image of Jesus Christ. Often, the results demand that I ask forgiveness, because my body betrayed me. It often expresses what I'm really thinking, even though my words may have been neutral. I'm working on it—all the time. What I'm learning is that when it is all about me, not others, I'm in danger of causing more hurt than healing. The questions that follow this chapter will ask you to consider those issues you must take captive in your own behavior.

HEALING OTHERS

All sorts of people can inspire and motivate others to bring about change. Members of the so-called Mafia certainly can motivate change. Dictators do. School bullies do. Revolutionaries revolt and inspire many others to do the same.

Sometimes, the oasis of hoped-for change is just a mirage. When the "going gets tough," those claiming leadership recognition, even some espousing servant-leadership, respond and react in ways that are not consistent with emotional healing. The practice of seeking righteousness in that leader (as the basis for developing an authentic *serving-leader attitude*— no matter your leadership style) produces the kind of changes that bring healing and real hope to followers, because "the mouth of the righteous is a well of life."[155] Leaders, drawing from a well of "living water," are equipped to motivate people by quenching their thirst with "the healing water" from the Giver of Life. This provides real hope in the midst of an ever-changing world—even the world of the workplace. This kind of motivation for healing is not a result of proselytizing; it is the result of *practicing* the kind of talk—speech—that reflects Jesus Christ in you.

In a current model of servant-leadership, the authors recognize something they call "Antecedent Conditions," the second of which is "leader attributes."[156] They have identified something in the servant-leader that changes how the behaviors they acknowledge are lived out. From a Christian perspective, that antecedent condition expresses a personal righteousness by means of the righteousness of Jesus Christ and is not based on our own works or our own wishes. We discipline ourselves for Christ so that we can inspire others to want what we have—which is our expression of God's peace reigning in our hearts and minds.[157] This is the attitude change we seek.

According to Kotter,[158] a leader sets the direction, aligns the key factors that will yield success, motivates and inspires, and produces positive change. To do these things, words take on great power. If a leader's words are colored by discouragement and by hesitancy based on current circumstances and an almost fatalistic recognition of present conditions, motivation is lost. Followers are not inspired. There is no joy, for the leader's words are not drawn from the "well of life." Even in the midst of tragedy, economic hardship, and loss, the *serving-leader attitude* will yield a reliance on the love of God and His concern about developing our character in our response to the conditions. Developing positive responses to negative circumstances motivates and inspires. Setting direction and aligning—to move from the current state to a future state—sometimes takes wisdom beyond human understanding. Like Job of old, we must rely on the goodness of God.

Leaders recognize that economies and businesses have sunny summers of success and cold winters of deadness and slowness. Leading is the process of behaving well despite the circumstance, reflecting a discipline to respond appropriately, not react emotionally. Regardless of *your* season, the personal focus *must be* on how the Lord is showing up even if you are in the "winter of your discontent."[159] Christian leaders must first communicate *joy*—*because* the "joy of the Lord is your strength."[160] Effective leaders speak first of what is going well (in a church or ministry context, it would be a conversation about God's goodness) *before* they communicate the trials that must be faced and overcome. We can only truly motivate and inspire when we draw first from the "well of life," so the bucket of words drawn will contain words chosen carefully and spoken with wisdom: again, words that heal. The *serving-leader attitude* understands that words based on The Word can bring about change, and they also understand that "rash language cuts and maims, but there is healing in the words of the wise."[161]

COMMITMENT TO PERSONAL CHANGE

Leading change demands the leader commit to personal behavioral change. Positive change in our relationships with others takes intentionality. People are sometimes "destroyed" by what is said and how it is said, as they spontaneously react negatively to the change. The wise leader recognizes the various impacts of change on the team and *carefully* chooses and speaks words that heal by creating value and meaning for each person experiencing the change. That leader chooses how to express the direction of change as well as when and how to align the key factors necessary to accomplish that change. Leading is not about being a bull in a china shop!

In his book *Leadership Without Easy Answers,* Harvard professor Ronald Heifetz posits that the role of leadership is changing. The new role is "to push us to clarify *our values* [emphasis mine] and face hard realities and to seize new possibilities however frightening they may be."[162] Facing hard realities is difficult at best, but made more productive when the words and attitudes chosen reflect a mindset of serving before leading. The team buy-in is easier when it is congruent with shared values. New possibilities can be imagined when content of the words spoken are in sync with tone of voice and body language (which communicates *more* than the words spoken). Personal change is sometimes painful, but must be endured, because the leader's journey will yield positive changes in his or her relationships with followers.

Crosby, in his book *The Absolutes of Leadership*, describes five leadership personalities:

- "Destructors—sees things only from their own perspective;
- Procrastinators—waste people's time and energy;
- Caretakers—are frozen in time;
- Preparers—plan well but are inflexible; and
- Accomplishers—through words and deeds inspire, motivate all stakeholders to move the organization ahead."[163]

What is interesting is that the communication styles move along a continuum that is similar to the personalities listed above. The "Destructor" will use rash language that cuts and maims, while the "Accomplisher" is a wise communicator who brings healing to customers, suppliers and employees, so that all are building positive relationships within the business. Business strategy is virtually meaningless until the leader successfully motivates the team to change. Motivation is the predicate of healing words, words that build and do not destroy, words that inspire personal change in behavior for the benefit of the individual and the organization. A *serving-leader attitude* strives to be the "accomplisher," because this attitude recognizes that "those who control their tongue will have a long life; opening your mouth can ruin everything."[164]

People learning to practice a *serving-leader attitude* control their behavior. They recognize the various impacts of change on the team and carefully choose and speak words that heal by creating value and meaning for each person experiencing the change. Controlling your behavior takes work and consistent effort. It starts with a willingness to submit to the little things in life.

R. C. Sproul tells the story of riding with a friend in his neighborhood filled with stop signs that virtually everyone ignored. His buddy, a Christian, was driving and coasted through a stop sign. When R. C. asked if he had seen it, his buddy confirmed he had and then added, "Yes, but I'm not going to let a bit of tin with red and white paint control my behavior."[165]

Like many options written about in this book, you have a choice: either practice controlling behavior by being willing to "submit yourselves for the Lord's sake to every human authority…"[166] or by simply ignoring the inconvenient rules—since it's all about you anyway. The question is what is the bit of tin with some red and white paint in your life that you tend to ignore? What are you going to do about it? The following questions may help reveal the "bits of tin" in your life.

CHAPTER 9 QUESTIONS

Question 44: What behaviors of yours need to be addressed?

Question 45: What tools might you use to help control those behaviors?

Question 46: What mental discipline do you need to develop so your words result in joy, hope and inspiration to bring about positive change?

Question 47: In what particular ways do you behave that have a healing effect on others?

Question 48: How do your particular behavioral/personality strengths impact people in your life?

What produces powerful results? What does not and what do you need to do to change that? (Your choice: discuss in the context of your team, your best friends, or your marriage.)

Question 49: How do you create value in your community—and what do you intentionally "give back?"

Question 50: What are the negative impacts that may emerge when you use too much of your "strengths"?

What you are going to do to learn to moderate them?

Section IV:
GIVING YOURSELF

"Everybody can be great...because anybody can serve. You don't have to have a college degree to serve. You don't have to make your subject and verb agree to serve. You only need a heart full of grace. A soul generated by love."

Martin Luther King, Jr.

Chapter 10:
Giving Yourself: Motivation

"I came to serve, not be served."

Jesus Christ

PEOPLE MATTER

Giving one's self grows out of a conviction that people matter. It must be difficult to rationalize the dignity of the individual when one believes that randomness and lifeless chemicals gave rise to people. I have yet to meet a dignified chemical or a bolt of lightning that has dignity.[167] The model I'm proposing in order to develop an authentic *serving-leader attitude* posits that the process starts with knowing yourself in particular ways and then learning to control yourself before you can begin really *giving* yourself. "Purity is best demonstrated by generosity."[168] That's what Jesus said to a group of religious people who thought their practice of religion would make them pure before God. These people were not some outliers of religious belief, either; they were practicing the major faiths of that day. The problem was this: they were counting on their own ability to be kind, generous, and compassionate. That's "nice," but it is not what God asks. He wants purity to produce generosity, and that purity does not come from inside us. Instead, it is given to us when we obey God.

In this section of the book, we will explore how the *serving-leader attitude* grows out of knowing and controlling yourself with God's help, resulting in a life that is developing the character traits that deliver purity. The picture is that we are to clothe ourselves with these *giving* traits by putting them on. This speaks of an act of our will: "*So, chosen by God for this new life of love, dress in the wardrobe God picked out for you: compassion, kindness, humility, quiet strength, discipline. Be even-tempered, content with second place, quick to forgive an offense. Forgive as quickly and completely as the Master forgave you. And regardless of what else you put on, wear love. It's your basic, all-purpose garment. Never be without it.*"[169] So, as you consider *giving yourself* by motivating others, sharing passion and being humble, consider each of these attributes as clothes that must be put on. And just as you don't wear the same clothes to bed as you do in your waking hours, these clothes must be put on each day, or motivation will look like manipulation. Passion will look like narcissism, and humility will look like self-righteousness.

MOTIVATING OTHERS

Leading by its very nature necessitates followers. Motivating those followers involves "a serious meddling in other people's lives."[170] Done well, all within a Christ-honoring context, this meddling produces the kind of motivation that can drive successful change management. People want to feel liberated to work well. In fact, my friend and colleague Deborah Brazeal, in her new book, *The New Business Paradigm: A Christian's Worldview in a Secular Marketplace*, finds it "fascinating that the results most business leaders crave are firmly and empirically rooted in Christian doctrine... In fact, the research demonstrates that the experience of working in a company with Christian values is so freeing and liberating to employee members (including the CEO's and executives themselves) that they feel motivated to perform."[171]

The previous fifty questions should have helped you understand the role that your relationship with Jesus Christ plays in how well you know yourself and control yourself, and the twenty questions that remain will begin to shape how you give yourself in a particular leadership role. Motivating others to perform can be a gift, if given well. Brazeal also noted that "[T]here is greater consensus that work should provide spiritual and personal growth as well as financial gain and that employees at all levels are more motivated when their souls are nourished."[172] It is my prayer that in answering the questions at the end of this chapter, you will begin to nourish yourself so you can share that nourishment with others.

YOU ARE TODAY BECAUSE OF WHAT YOU WERE THEN

When teaching at the university level, it is interesting to see the difference between those with military training and those without. Students with a military background are bringing to the assignments a different kind of motivation and a sense of proportionality than those without that training. They motivate others in the group in ways that produce better group results. They have a better sense of their core values. They know how to motivate by realizing there are times when they need to show dominance, to show the willingness to step-up and lead and to demonstrate that they are doing it for the good of the group, not themselves. Even in my business career, working with retired military in the Silicon Valley was different in tone and quality from working with those who did not have that background.

Retired Colonel John Lowry, currently the General Manager at Harley-Davidson, points out that "the people you are serving with come from all walks of life; the military is this great purely merit-based institution in our society. Learning how to deal with anybody—wherever they come from—is something that I leverage today in business when dealing with my suppliers and customers."[173]

There is another key: how you show up and how you *are* in situations where you need to step up. Your attitude makes all the difference, because "a cheerful disposition is good for your health [and your team's]; gloom and doom leave you [and your team] bone-tired."[174] The principle: what is good for you is also good for the health of your team.

Health professionals have long recognized this truth, but it is now permeating the business community. According to author Susan Heathfield, writing on employee motivation, a leader should "start the day by showing a positive, cheerful attitude. (Your arrival at work sets the employee motivation tone for the day.)"[175] Good medicine for you is good medicine for those around you at school, at work, at home. Those practicing a *serving-leader attitude* lay the foundation for the culture one genuine smile and pleasant disposition at a time.

Why we do what we do says more about our character than what we do. Our motivations are often hidden—sometimes even from us. Leadership that is self-centered is limiting. According to authors Porras, Emery and Thompson, leadership that succeeds over time is attributable to the strength of the cause they pursue: "Enduringly successful people serve the cause—and they are lifted up by its power."[176] Motivating others to follow and succeed and then become leaders themselves are major threads in the tapestry of the *serving-leader attitude*. In his article "What Leaders Really Do," Kotter observes that "well-led businesses tend to recognize and reward people who successfully develop leaders." [177]

An arrogant-leadership-attitude does not develop followers who become leaders; its motivations, often hidden from public view, are self-centered and limiting. Those leaders practicing a *serving-leader attitude* will motivate others and succeed over time because of the strength of the causes they pursue. Here are two transforming causes to pursue:

- Find and *control* the motivations that are just about you.
- Feed and *nurture* the motivations that are about helping and building-up others.

PRAISE WILL TEST A LEADER'S MOTIVATIONS

When leaders communicate, they reveal much about themselves, especially their authenticity. When providing sales training, I've noticed that some trainees want to adopt certain perceived personality traits, thinking those traits will make a person a better sales representative. Not so. Lack of authenticity is soon detected. Whether an analytic, a driver, an expressive or amiable sales person (like a leader), one must root their communication in authenticity. While they may learn to effectively communicate in a manner consistent with the receiver's communication style, they must do this from a motivation of helping others, not *manipulating* them. In the learning of that skill, authenticity purifies the messages delivered.

We all like to hear "Job well done!" How we hear it and who is telling us are both critical to our ability to process the communication. When pricked with praise, we bleed humility. You cannot do that if you are faking it. Those who are committed to developing a *serving-leader attitude* will be able to respond to the test of praise with honesty and gratitude, appreciative of the praise, but not gloating in it. By such behavior, they motivate those following to be open to praise.

Your followers also like to hear praise. When you praise them sincerely, you can begin to gain insight into their hearts. Some issues to look for include:

- Do they accept praise graciously or do they shrug it off as if it is not important?
- Do they swell up inappropriately, showing that pride or arrogance is creeping out at the edges?
- Do they give credit where credit is due? (Is that authentic or simply dressing up a lack of self-confidence?)

Praise is a powerful management tool. It reveals much. Those working on developing an authentic, Kingdom-driven *serving-leader attitude* must daily empty self to allow the Spirit to move in. Discipline is involved. Commitment to the *final praise* from the Almighty ("Well done, good and faithful servant"[178]) must drive us. (See Question #4 again.)

Followers—motivated by leaders who express character, compassion, concern and conviction—produce results that catch the attention and praise of those watching. How the leader handles that adulation the first time will predict whether a second time will result.

PERFORMANCE WILL TEST A LEADER'S ABILITY TO MOTIVATE

Not everybody performs to expectation. Often it is a mismatch between a required skill set and the skill set of the employee or team member. The LIFO® methodology recommended earlier in this book is a tool that can better match people to the skills needed to perform a job. An existing body of research shows that many firms are able to motivate well and therefore enjoy a maximum level of engagement in the business. But a problem still lingers: for many of those companies where leaders motivate well, there is a lingering sense of missing the mark in terms of producing expected performance results. If the leader makes assumptions not based on a clear understanding of the skills, bent, and inclinations of the team members to do a job well, the results produced may not meet expectations. "That is, motivation to contribute has to be matched with the ability to contribute."[179]

Brazeal tells a story about Jose, an entrepreneur who helped a friend with independent contract work. However, there was a mismatch that eventually led to firing his friend. How Jose managed that interaction clearly represents someone who has learned God's way of leading.

"Jose subscribes to the notion that everyone is uniquely created with God-given talents that are equally respectful and credible. 'Firing' someone is necessary if the set of skills do not match the specific task. Thus, if a job calls for analytical skills and a considerable amount of financial analysis and the contracted colleague is actually high in team-building or collaborative skills, then there is no judgment about which set of skills is better. Jose praises his colleague for the skill set he does have and leads his colleague to the understanding that this is simply a case of skills not matching the job. There is no judgment nor is firing a reflection of the individual's intellectual capacity. In this fashion, the colleague (and friend) can retain dignity and remain a friend. Too often, this scenario would be played out in a demeaning manner where the colleague feels incompetent or even ignorant and leaves feeling demoralized."[180]

MOTIVATION IS AN ATTITUDE, NOT A RESULT OF AUTHORITY

Motivation is not positional authority. Titles are not relevant. Some, even without a title that suggests power or position, become skilled at motivating those around them, sometimes even those above them. A *serving-leader attitude* is not one's position on the organizational chart. Instead, it derives its inspiration from being an authentic Christ-follower who derives power from knowing, controlling and giving. The authority to motivate results from a combination of at least five skills (there may be others, but these I have found to be transformational):

- Developing interpersonal power (understanding behaviors)
- Pointing to a direction
- Leading by *being*, not just *doing*
- Listening—actively
- Practicing empathy

These skills are developed by intentionality; they are not natural to humans, especially the skill of active listening. Developing a *serving-leader attitude* involves listening as an activity of one's ears, mind, eyes, undivided attention and heart. Much activity takes effort. It involves discipline of intentionality. The Chinese language, which uses characters to paint word pictures, gives some insight into their wisdom regarding listening. The symbol on the left side represents the ear. Top right is the person, below the "+" sign are the eyes of the mind and underneath are "undivided attention" and the "heart." We listen with both ears, maintain eye contact while giving the speaker our undivided attention, and become empathetic. Notice how this form of listening builds the framework for the last two items in the five-point skills list above. The combination produces some insights worth consideration. First, focus on understanding the person speaking *before* you seek to be understood. It is hard to listen with understanding while framing your next reply, so focus not only on the words said, but also on the language of the body and the tone of the voice. These last two say much if one pays attention. Making judgments about what the speaker is saying gets in the way of listening with understanding. I freely admit this is tough to learn and even harder to practice on an ongoing basis. If one is going to motivate, one must first understand without determining a judgment about what is being said. However, if one is focused on developing a clear understanding about the speaker's frame of reference, when it is time to reply, the words will be more motivational. After all, people love applause—that's why many perform—so this is an apt metaphor for a listener to provide positive feedback to a speaker (even when there might be disagreement about the subject). Feedback says, "I hear what you are saying..." or "I'm beginning to understand your point-of-view about this subject..." Such feedback will go a long way in motivating others when change from what has been to what will be is needed.

It is the Chinese heart symbol, though, that is so very instructive. Throughout this book, I have talked about the right attitude, the right mind-set and the right kind of self-talk. I've talked about the "heart," which encompasses both our mind and our spirit and which speaks to us in ways we must *hear* to understand. Too often, the mind kicks into gear and engages the tongue to speak before the heart is connected to the conversation. This is why the marvelous magic of motivation springs from a heart that has the right attitude, even about listening.

In their book *Whale Done*, the authors posit that motivating change results, at its core, from accentuating the positive behavior and ignoring and redirecting the negative behaviors, all done in a trusting environment that pays more attention to the behavior you want repeated and less to the behavior that does not meet expectation. To change behavior, the authors suggest that better results will surface when the leader varies the positive rewards. Predictability in rewards changes the flow of learning. If the "trainers" of killer whales can develop tools to motivate a change in behavior, perhaps we ought to take some notice.

Begin by developing the habit of "catching people doing things right!"[181] Positive change will result. People will be motivated to do what is right when that produces praise—a keystone of building trust and producing great results. Ralph Waldo Emerson is quoted as saying, "Trust men and they will be true to you. Trust them greatly and they will show themselves great." As Meyer and Slechta remind us, "worthy leaders" motivate people even unto death. They tell the story of Spartacus, who escaped from his slavery taking seventy followers with him as he led an insurrection against Rome. After he and his troops defeated legions, the Emperor Crassus had had enough and managed to crush the rebellion. In the battle, Spartacus was killed, but the legions did not know that. They believed him alive and hiding in the captured masses. When questioned by the Romans, each follower of Spartacus proudly proclaimed, "I am Spartacus!" The Romans, frustrated with each making that proclamation, crucified all of them.[182]

It is this kind of trust and motivation that one practicing development of the *serving-leader attitude* instills in followers. By giving of themselves, these kind of leaders prove that the "emotional healing," the "empowering," the commitment to "helping followers grow and succeed" are indeed real behaviors worthy of people following—even to the death. These kinds of leaders and followers truly "create value for the community."[183]

The following ten questions will help you shape a positive attitude from which to motivate.

CHAPTER 10 QUESTIONS

Question 51: How do you demonstrate that you are committed to clear, consistent, compelling and constant communication about core values and behaviors?

Consider also the elements of active listening that you want to develop.

Question 52: How do you motivate others?

Write about how you adapt to different personality styles, what is working and what is not, and what you will change in the latter.

Question 53: How do you intentionally serve someone who may look to you as a leader?

Question 54: How are you demonstrating inspirational leadership not just in words, but also by consistent actions?

Think in terms of specific examples.

Question 55: What specific tools do you use to train others in a way that inspires them?

Question 56: How do you align yourself with the culture of a team and contribute fully to it?

Question 57: In what specific ways will the tools you use to align, motivate and inspire be supported by Scripture?

Question 58: What tools do you use with your team to help guide direction?

Question 59: What are some of the most difficult issues you face in applying these tools?

Question 60: When you must discipline someone, what are the steps you take to prepare yourself and them?

How might you discipline your followers and still glorify Jesus Christ?

Chapter 11:
Giving Yourself: Passion

"I came to serve, not be served."

Jesus Christ

CHRISTIAN WORLDVIEW MOTIVATES PASSION

Christ-followers are free people. After all, redemption, forgiveness, love, goodness and mercy always free people. People who enjoy freedom are not fearful of expressing passion. Passionate people propel organizations. One leadership author states, "People grow toward the giver of energy, the giver of credit and affirmation. They flourish as persons when they receive affirmation."[184] In organizations where the Christian worldview predominates, employees flourish. Brazeal's research demonstrates this concept:

> *"Through an application of the Christian Worldview in the workplace, a culture emerges that encourages and practices: autonomy, an open door policy, safety, and a true team environment. Employees feel empowered to follow their God-given purpose through increased feasibility, or self-efficacy, meaning they have the capability and confidence to lead a balanced, harmonious work life. Additionally, employees become more passionate about their organizational role leading to greater performance, creativity and organizational commitment."* [185]

Tom Peters discovered this fact years ago in his research, and he noted that "top-flight performance is not dry and deadly; it is spirited; it is emotion-filled."[186] The passion of a leader's followers is directly related to his/her trust in the leader. One consultant in the field believes "people need an incredibly high level of freedom and trust in [a leader's] response before they'll release the passion that can lead to exceptional achievement." [187] God's laws, like principles of leadership, are fundamentally about two issues: personal integrity and the value of others. The *serving-leader attitude* is one that nourishes the care of others. "The greatest privilege of leadership is the chance to elevate lives." [188] That is an awesome responsibility. I know that I'm more naturally inclined to elevate *my* life, and our culture reinforces that kind of thinking. Sports and entertainment have both become more about the person than the team that supports and helps that person succeed. To elevate others, you have to know where they currently are in order to understand where they want and need to go. Those who purport to lead and "fail"—who don't produce the results they expected—miss the mark, because they don't understand *who it is* they're trying to lead—which takes competency, intimacy, integrity, and passion. It takes passion to know what is most precious: not the stuff that must be done, but the people who do it.

For the Christian leader who wants to give to others, I'm reminded of one of my mentor's favorite passages: "Never be lacking in zeal, but keep your spiritual fervor, serving the Lord."[189] In published comments, he challenges leaders who wish to serve by saying they "should be motivated by spiritual fervor… As Christians we are basically in the business of serving others because we are servants of the King, Jesus Christ."[190]

A MODEL FOR PASSION

Passion is not a monolithic concept. It is thought by some to be a critical element in the expression of talent and skill (like an artist or athlete). Martha Graham has noted that "great dancers are not great because of their technique; they are great because of their passion."[191] Descartes (1596-1650) noted that passions are strong emotions that can be positive as long as a person bases them on underlying reason.[192] Hegel (1770-1831) proclaimed that passion was necessary in high levels of achievement—"Nothing great in the world has ever been accomplished without passion."[193] I think we probably can see and can all agree that passion and achievement are related. Yet "he only employs his passion who can make no use of his reason," warns Marcus Tullius Cicero.[194] The bottom line is that passion is not directly related to thinking prowess, but it is a complex emotional fuel that can feed the engine of competitive excellence.

The history of the word *passion* provides some additional interesting insight. From an online dictionary reference, we learn that there is this underlying element of *suffering* that exists in the word *passion*.

> **Origin:** 1125—75; Middle English (< Old French) < Medieval Latin passiōn- (stem of passiō) Christ's sufferings on the cross, any of the Biblical accounts of these (> late Old English passiōn), special use of Late Latin passiō suffering, submission, derivative of Latin passus, past participle of patī to suffer, submit...[195]

This is certainly true for athletes who know there is a suffering that must be endured to physically excel. The same can be said for mental excellence: there is pressure and a sense of total submission to a process to immerse one's self in knowledge, thinking, studying, meditation and expression of what is learned. Submission: you saw that word, didn't you? Passion is something to which we could become enslaved—whether it's chocolate, crossword puzzles or cricket—if we don't maintain a balanced life.

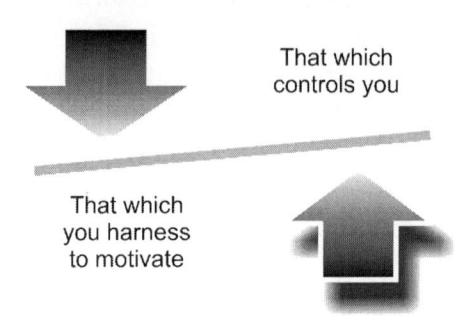

```
        ↓  That which
           controls you
    ─────────────
    That which    ↑
    you harness
    to motivate
```

A picture of passion

There is a body of research on passion and the values it brings to organizations. In some of that reading, I found an interesting dualism proposed by Vallerand & Houlfourt,[196] postulating that passion, expressed at work, consists of two distinctive types: the one is *obsessive* (not used pejoratively—just observationally, but with a warning), and the other is *harmonious* passion.

Obsessive passion occurs when one is pushed to achieve by internal forces—often not entirely consciously. This obsessive passion is the kind that drives some Olympic athletes to sacrifice so much in order to achieve a limited sense of perfection within their sport. However, this kind of focused obsession, especially at work, can control a person who therefore may become co-dependent on his or her work. My experience of life has revealed that co-dependence on anything is never a good thing.

Harmonious passion also has two characteristics according to Vallerand and Houlfourt. The first is a motivational force that leads to work activities one wants to see done well. The other is harmony with all aspects of one's life (one therefore exhibits a work/life balance).

Although I found this reading interesting, what I am proposing is that developing a *serving-leader attitude* is a useful combination of both to forge something I call *constructive passion.*™

The power of passion in leading consists of three elements I call the ABC's of Constructive Passion. For constructive passion to produce positive results while you're practicing your *serving-leader attitude*, you must *avoid, benefit* and *construct*.

A

Avoid connecting passion with the worth of any individual. Achievement is simply the consequence of excellence in a particular field, but that excellence is *not* the person. I see excellence expressed with four distinctive drivers, based on the LIFO® orientation values system:

1. Excellent at finding opportunity,
2. Excellent at analyzing information,
3. Excellent at creating harmony, and
4. Excellent at shaping the ideal.

We have already learned that people may have one or more of these passions for excellence, which should be seen as traits that God has designed in them for His glory. We each bring strengths to the table. Constructive passion recognizes those strengths and sees the combinations that best can be utilized to solve problems when managing complexity or leading change.

B

Benefit from the diversity of passions. Leaders look for and build teams around those who bring diverse passions, because different passions produce different kinds of achievements, including at least four perspectives:

- Passion for systems,
- Passion for action,
- Passion for helping, and
- Passion for negotiating.

C

Construct multiple opportunities for team members to stretch themselves, which sometimes involves using their least preferred, or natural, style to accomplish work tasks. There are four distinctive areas one could work on developing, and these include the following:

- Passion for filling the needs of others first,
- Passion for thinking before acting,
- Passion for being competent and seizing opportunity, and
- Passion for working hard and pursuing the ideal way.

However, one caution: it is difficult, if not impossible, to practice constructive passion without a clear sense of purpose. That passion includes both the internal drives God has put inside you and the learned behavior that benefits others. In combination, they provide real value to the organization. A believer's purpose must be to glorify God in everything s/he does. Developing sensitivity toward constructive passion can help in that journey.

PASSION, PRACTICE AND PERSISTENCE

The saying "practice makes perfect" is not exactly correct. Actually, it's "perfect practice makes 'perfect.'" When I think of practice, I think of the Olympics as the quintessential representation of the commitment to thousands of hours needed for those athletes to perfect a skill. This is especially true in gymnastics where virtuosity counts for so much of the routines: virtuosity is that quality of execution that evokes the observation that "I've seen that done a hundred times, but never so effortlessly and with such great precision." Passion fuels the engine of commitment to persist in practicing over and over again until the skill becomes part of the soul of the performer. The technical ability is woven into the fabric of the performance, despite the many mistakes that produced the kind of learning needed to conquer.

The past can damage passion. Let me illustrate it with font size. If your past looks like this to you, then your passion will look like this, and your anxiety level will be substantive.

Past Passion **Anxiety**

If, however, like great athletes, you are learning to use the mistakes of the past to fuel what you are doing in the present, then the perspectives change. The problem here is that your passion can become your idol and your past and the anxiety it brings still is lurking. People often substitute a passion for God. It becomes the focus. You become passionate about hiking, hunting, helping—whatever—and you leave God out of the picture. The present is not dominated by the past, passion is allowed to flourish, and anxiety about mistakes is overcome. How? With the passion to persist in perfect practice, you begin to focus on producing a perfect passion. This passion is not bad, evil or wrong, per se: it becomes a problem when it replaces God.

Past **Passion** Anxiety

For Christ-followers, there is yet another picture that enhances passion. It focuses on things that matter and provides a perspective people find attractive, because the person, surrounded by a God-reality, practices passion with a peace that is beyond human comprehension.

There arises a problem, even for Christ-followers: knowing yourself and controlling yourself require a daily surrender; when that does not happen, the picture changes. The vertical relationship with God may still exist, but the horizontal relationship with others is damaged when the *past* is given a foothold to control your passion and cause personal anxiety. The cure? Prayer and thanksgiving: *"Do not be anxious about anything, but in every situation, by prayer and petition, with thanksgiving, present your requests to God. And the peace of God, which transcends all understanding, will guard your hearts and your minds in Christ Jesus."*[197]

Your passion, surrounded by consciousness of your Creator, will produce in you a wholehearted devotion to not only love Him, but also love others in a way that meaningfully helps them to grow, be nurtured, and ultimately succeed in their jobs.

The word "God" is grayed back for a reason: a *serving-leader attitude* is not about wearing God on one's sleeve in a "Bible-thumping" sort of way. You want people to see your passion, but you want it to be an expression of Christ-like qualities: you may be the only expression of God's love that some people ever see. Let your passion be a heavenly expression of The Great Commandment.[198] God is greater than your past and greater than any anxiety. We all have pasts, and we all get anxious; only our utter dependence on God will yield a change in our attitude about each.

Often, our passion is a gift from God, but it may lie fallow without constant "stirring up." The Apostle Paul had to remind Timothy to *"stir up that inner fire which God gave you at your ordination. For God has not given us a spirit of fear, but a spirit of power and love and a sound mind."*[199] That "inner fire," that passion dedicated to God, is attractive, because it comes without fear; it comes in power that can transform. This passion shared should be encouraging, even in the midst of a negative environment.

When I was consulting with companies about their selling at national trade shows (back in the day), I would warn them of the weariness that comes from standing on a hard floor all day, and I would encourage them to work at *smiling* while standing. The smile relaxes. It is inviting. We would work on "inside jokes" that could be started with a spoken word that would help remind the booth workers to smile.

For the Christian, life is like working a trade show all the time. The "joy of the Lord" must be our strength. I find this sometimes difficult, because I can easily get so wrapped up in myself. I don't always produce joy. I know it is tough. Part of spiritual discipline involves allowing God to live through you; as John the Baptist commented about his life, "He must become greater and greater and I must become less and less."[200] There it is! That's the secret. Passion expressed as an outpouring of the Spirit of God living in you will do a work that manufactured passion will never duplicate.

WHOLEHEARTED PASSIONATE LEADING

Passionate leading changes people. It changes the mundane into the marvelous by seeing potential others miss. It drives commitment that fulfills the promises made. It provides the energy to solve what seems insurmountable. The Apostle Paul put it this way: "*That means you must not give sin a vote in the way you conduct your lives. Don't give it the time of day. Don't even run little errands that are connected with that old way of life. Throw yourselves wholeheartedly and full-time—remember, you've been raised from the dead!—into God's way of doing things. Sin can't tell you how to live. After all, you're not living under that old tyranny any longer. You're living in the freedom of God.*"[201] Not much I can add. Passion's source from a soul changed by the living God will not only change you, but it also will change those around you. God wants our passion. People want our passion. For your passion to have a positive purpose though, it must find its source in our God who is passionate for His creation.

Helen Keller is quoted as saying, "Life is either a daring adventure or nothing at all." That's passion in the face of what many would consider problems. God has called all of us to live adventurous lives—abundant lives—lives filled with meaning. This kind of living is attractive to a world seeking peace, personal prosperity and power. As Meyer and Slechta point out, "Effective leaders possess passion that can be transmitted to others."[202] Passion must be shared to have meaning when living inside a *serving-leader attitude*.

Plato made an interesting observation in *The Republic*:

> "*When we say that a man desires something, do we say he desires all that pertains to it or only one part and not another?... Then any student who is half-hearted in his studies—especially when he is you and lacks the understanding to judge between what is useful and what is not—cannot be called...a lover of wisdom. He is like one who picks at his food. We say that he is not really hungry and has no appetite. We say that he is a poor eater and no lover of the table.*"[203]

Leaders must have passion about the *purpose* to which they are committed. Wholeheartedness powerfully moves people—it is *passion* personified. Followers love leaders who are committed with their heads (rational thinking) and their hearts (passion and compassion). A leader's passion coupled with knowledge that learning from results has produced (no labels—learning) are mixed in the cauldron of experience that, under the fires of change (and complexity), will yield a meal of confidence that will feed the spirit of those being led.

Joshua, of walls of Jericho fame, inherited the leadership reins from Moses. His side-kick Caleb—of whom it is said by God, "Because my servant Caleb has a different spirit and follows me *wholeheartedly*, I will bring him into the land he went to, and his descendants will inherit it"[204]—became Joshua's number two and helped Joshua lead Israel into the Promised Land. What a legacy! Joshua, a man filled with fear, overcame that fear to follow God with Caleb at his side. Caleb, who was willing to submit himself passionately to the authority of Joshua's leadership, is a positive example of one who showed a *serving-leader attitude*. We leaders need to find more Caleb-like colleagues within our teams!

That's exactly what we—leaders and followers—are called to do in the workplace: "Serve *wholeheartedly*, as if you were serving the Lord, not people."[205]

Adopting a *serving-leader attitude* is not a half-hearted exercise: you must be wholehearted in your study of God's way as written in His Word—the *textbook* of living, leadership and management. Don't pick and choose from the Word of God what you want when you want it. Instead, develop an appetite for leadership based on eternal principles, and an appetite requires consistent reading, meditating and learning from the greatest practitioner of a *serving-leading attitude* of all, Jesus Christ.[206]

PASSION'S PITFALLS

Love, like passion, must be shared to have meaning. If I say I love you and don't share any of myself with you, that is not love—those words are empty. In Chapter 1, I noted that Jesus warns us about empty words. Passion shared drives teams and organizations—the question is to what end.

Is passion always a positive force? No! Passion may be hidden, but it is always around, yet not necessarily always obvious. People may be polite, sweet, quiet and precise in their interactions with others, but behind that façade is a passion that, if expressed, would be explosive to interactions. People, like organizations, may wear masks, because they believe that passionate people are not grounded—or other myths. Bottom line: passion may be positive or negative, seen or hidden.[207]

Hidden, negative passions damage a leader's ability to motivate and inspire. Team members who have been harboring something that may have nothing to do with the leader, per se, may suddenly release that negative passion into the interaction. That's why the *serving-leader attitude* is built upon a spiritual foundation. The Evil One will use hidden, negative passions to sabotage a Christian leader's effectiveness. The Apostle Paul warns us that we don't battle against people—flesh and blood—but against power and unseen rulers of darkness. [208] The workplace for an authentic leader is a battlefield, and leadership must be armed with the armor of God.

Passion must be authentic—it must not be faked. When faced with impediments to a team's success, authentic passion will drive questions like the following:

- What are the impediments to success that must be overcome?
- What strengths do we possess that, if put to right uses, will help us overcome?
- What are team weaknesses that must be ameliorated to help us overcome any impediment?
- What are the rewards once the impediment is overcome—and are those rewards worth the effort?

Passion is different from wishful thinking. Passion drives change by being shared in such a way that risk-taking is not judged (success or failure), but is understood and results in learning. This kind of passion demands that a leader find positive passions that can be leveraged to solve business problems.

It is the leader's job to find the positive passions of people on the team and tap into that reservoir of energy and emotion. It will add shape and substance to the rational. It will help drive your team when the impediments seem insurmountable. The following five questions will help you assess your passion and develop an awareness and sensitivity to your team's passions.

CHAPTER 11 QUESTIONS

Questions 61: What is your passion?

Questions 62: What do you need to do to help you passionately live in the completed future—the "it is so" attitude?

Questions 63: How will you go about authentically sharing your passion?

Questions 64: In what ways can you direct your passion to help your "team" be joyful and fulfilled?

Questions 65: How are your passion and your purpose connected, and what insights emerge when working on this answer?

Chapter 12:
Giving Yourself: Humility

"I came to serve, not be served."

Jesus Christ

BE HUMBLE!

"For he who is least among you all—he is the greatest."[209] When Jesus laid down this humility gauntlet, the fight between the natural nature and the supernatural nature battle lines were clearly drawn. What humans in their sin nature naturally seek is greatness, not "leastness." We Americans especially, raised in a culture now several centuries old, are well schooled in working toward a "self-actualized" leadership style. Our movies extol the virtues of the quiet, strong, cowboy who saves the day and then rides off into the sunset. He does not want adulation. He does not want to become the sheriff. He wants to quietly move on.

Even modern versions of the old West cowboy have the same characteristics. We seem to have this drive to idolize the independent spirit that helps the helpless and wants nothing in return. We want that. We extol that. But in the heat of our normal battles, we seem to be a culture more comfortable wanting recognition for our leadership in the time of need.

Jesus' statement seems to be the antithesis of what one might assume to be an important leadership quality. Humility is often a misunderstood trait. Then again, is it a behavioral process? Jim Collins, in his seminal work on the attributes that have made great companies, discovered that humility plays a key role in defining great company leaders. They were cut from a cloth that combined both great personal humility and an equally great resoluteness of will.[210]

Not all writers agree on which is the best way to describe humility as a leadership attribute. I do know this: humility is accepting that God may want to change us rather than our circumstances. This is why humility is one of the three legs of *giving yourself* in the *serving-leader attitude* paradigm.

Humility is not looking for the "me" in the swirling events of life; it is learning to look for God at work in us. Humility is not looking for Him to explain events in a way that would satisfy us. Rather, He is looking for us to know Him better because of the circumstances. Why? He is more interested in our character than the conditions of any situation. He is interested in how we behave, because He wants each of us to develop the trait of humility by changing ourselves to be conformed to the image of Jesus Christ. That process of change begins with an attitude that holds fast to the reality that we are to "give thanks in all circumstances; for this is the will of God in Christ Jesus for you."[211]

Leaders who are willing to learn from circumstances will be able to attract followers. The leader needs followers. Those who follow need to feel that the leaders are authentic, that they are not always the smartest one in the room, and that they are willing to learn. It is clear that Scripture recognizes right-living (righteousness) as a trait focused on others by reminding us that "[t]he righteous is a guide to his neighbor."[212] Righteousness, at its core, includes the concept of a humble spirit. It represents a life that is distinctive from the normal pattern of living. Humility sets those practicing it apart from others.

One expert on leadership put it this way: "Want to demonstrate that you have what it takes to be an effective leader and have people follow your direction? Be humble!"[213]

KNOW WHERE TO SIT!

Baldoni, often quoted in the Harvard Business Review, says this directly and straightforwardly. The fact is, humility is not easily associated with leadership. Jesus made it starkly clear when he told a story with the theme of *know where to sit!* Telling his audience that running for the best seats in the house, and taking them, could be a humbling experience when the person in charge brings someone even more important than you to sit in the seat you thought "belonged" to someone of your stature. In fact, much of the literature on leadership, before Jim Collins' work in *Built to Last* and *Good to Great,* dismissed humility as nice for non-profit or church work, but ineffectual for the business community. Leaders sat up front, in the best seats, where leaders are expected to sit. Collins changed that point of view with his research, and both Baldoni and Collins have concluded that the combination of humility, vision and a "resoluteness of will" (Collins)—a backbone of steel—makes one a more effective leader.

Knowing where to sit involves the discipline of knowing what to say and when. I asked one of my mentors years ago why he had not engaged in an exchange with a client about the facts of a situation. His answer shocked me. "Griff, I don't need to let him know that I know more about it than he does; I just need to let him know that I'm listening to him and understanding his perspective." That was a revelation to me. I was raised to stand for "the truth" of a situation—despite who was expounding. He practiced a humble spirit, because it was about the client, not him. Arrogance, I learned, was all about me proving what I knew, and George taught me that, even at its best, trying to be the *smartest one in the room* is dishonest: no one knows everything.

The behavior of a Christian leader should reflect the combination of traits that balance abasement with positive attitude. The trait reflects that neither little regard for self nor much regard for self really operate well for leaders who want to attract followers. Secular writers in the field have noted that humility has three dimensions, which I discovered several years after developing this paradigm for a *serving-leader attitude*. Andrew Morris and others posited that effective leaders have the following qualities:

- **"Self-awareness**: *The ability to understand one's strength and weakness, getting real and staying real, not believing your own hype, and the ability to recognize and admit one's mistakes.*
- **"Openness**: *Recognizing one's limitations, being open to new ideas and knowledge and willingness to listen and learn from others, and having the ability to change. Being open means to encourage dissent and value truth over cover-ups, being willing to ask for and utilize the help of others.*
- **"Transcendence**: *The acceptance of something greater than the self. This leads one away from self-aggrandizement and self-benefiting behavior toward valuing and appreciating others and their opinions and ideas in the organization."*[214]

The behavior of the Christian leader should reflect that latter trait of transcendence, because integrating faith into the workplace is *not* about trying to convert anyone to a religion. It is behaving in such a way that non-believers become "men and women of character who recognize that they are not the center of the universe…who treat everybody with dignity and respect because we've all been created in the image of God."[215] They do this not only by what they say, but also by what they do—better said, how "they show up" in any human interaction. Remember, "humility… is not thinking less of yourself; it's thinking about yourself less."[216] If Christian leaders have worked through *knowing* themselves and *controlling* themselves, then integrating faith in the workplace is about a combination of actions and words expressed humbly. Of course, it's easier to write than do, I'll admit, but it becomes more and more of a behavior once one's worldview in the workplace is shaped by the realization that we are Ambassadors for God at work. Then again, as Pearcey points out, "Unless they are submitting themselves to a continual process of sanctification, they will not have the power to live out that worldview—and they will discredit the very message they are seeking to communicate."[217]

OBEDIENCE AND HUMILITY

A *serving-leader attitude* demands that leaders "live in harmony by showing love for each other... [They are not] jealous or proud, but [are] humble and consider others more important than themselves. [They] care about them as much as [they] care about [themselves] and think the same way that Christ Jesus thought: Christ was truly God. But he did not try to remain equal with God. Instead he gave up everything and became a slave, when he became like one of us. Christ was humble. He obeyed God and even died on a cross."[218]

The foundation of humility is simple: obedience. The admonition from the Apostle Paul includes the thought that we are to have the "same mindset"[219]—the same attitude as Jesus Christ. The Christian business leaders in secular marketplaces must demonstrate an attitude that is strikingly different from those around them. Their concern for their followers or employees or team members must be an expression of something palatable. They are more likely to share credit and take blame, since they are not working for themselves or the company, but they know they are working to please God in every decision. "What would Jesus do?" constantly plays in their minds as they manage complexity and lead the change needed to move ahead. Again, based on my experience, this is easier to write than it is to do. This is a daily journey for the Christ-follower and demands a certain discipline to be in His Word on a daily basis.[220]

SHOWING HONOR

If one is authentic—without pretense or arrogance—one then can become devoted to followers by removing roadblocks, by making certain they have the tools they need to achieve what the company needs, and by doing other tangible things to help them "get stuff done." The *serving-leader attitude* honors the team by giving credit to the team members who accomplished the work on behalf of the leader and by being willing to take the blame when things go wrong, especially when results may have been beyond the control of the follower. A *serving-leader attitude* facilitates accepting *blame*, because a responsibility of leaders is their ability to see consequences—to look for unintended consequences and protect the followers from them. This attitude honors people. The Apostle Paul provides some insight: "Be devoted to one another in brotherly love; give preference to one another in honor."[221] One translator renders the thought this way: "Love from the center of who you are; don't fake it. Run for dear life from evil; hold on for dear life to good. Be good friends who love deeply; practice playing second fiddle."[222] That attitude is committed to the success of peers, subordinates and bosses. Honor must not be sought—only bestowed. If and when the leader practicing a *serving-leader attitude* receives honor, that leader will know the source and be thankful to the One who used people to bless her or him with words that honor. The principle is an old one Joshua learned when he began to lead the ancient nation of Israel: "Then the LORD said to Joshua, 'Today I will begin to honor you in front of all the people of Israel. I will do this to let them know that I am with you just as I was with Moses.'"[223] This is the kind of honor that matters most!

PRACTICE PLAYING SECOND FIDDLE

Practice playing second fiddle? How does a leader do *that?* "Do" may not be the correct verb. It is an attitude, not necessarily a box on an organizational chart. That is, it is not something you do—it is who you are. It is a way of thinking about those working for you, or for those on your team. It is remembering that, as a leader developing a *serving-leader attitude,* you shouldn't "worry if people don't recognize your merits; [instead] worry that you may not recognize theirs."[224] It is looking at others in such a way that they are empowered by the authentic sense of the leader's care for them, not by some manipulation of potential extrinsic rewards.

The essence of empowerment is motivation. To succeed motivating in a meaningful way, one must learn to use both extrinsic and intrinsic drivers. I call them the *5 M's of Motivating*.

MOTIVES: providing opportunities for achievement for power and for affiliation (being on the inside). These *extrinsic* drivers are those that are most naturally touched; by themselves, however, they are weak.

MOMENT: emphasizing the environment (office location, cubicle location, etc.), culture (the rising team—the winning team), job characteristics (working on the best, newest, most important). Often it's the current situation. This is another *extrinsic* driver that is used as the motivation for change. It's okay in some instances, but doesn't go deep.

MIND: a set of cognitive choices like incentives, expectations and status. This is the "ultimate" *extrinsic* corporate motivation driven by MBA-based thinking. But the cognitive choices are often fleeting and transient and by themselves offer only temporary motivation, since they still don't touch what's inside the person.

MOVEMENT: *intrinsic* emotional choices of preferences; enjoyment, challenges, and being part of a team are at the "heart" of motivation. Here you begin to touch the passion of individuals and move them to tap into how they can best capitalize on their values, goals, behavioral drivers and beliefs. It is putting them in the best position to succeed based on who they *are*.

ME: our *way of being* is another *intrinsic* motivation that taps into the heart and passion of a person and his or her humility. If you have created a climate that encourages teamwork, initiative, and decision-making, you will not be caught in the valley of the-lack-of-enthusiastic-participation in the leader's plan. Instead, you will have made a heart connection and given them passion that is washed in righteousness and modeled with humility.

Even Machiavelli recognized the power of esteem when he wrote that a leader should give "recognition to virtuous men, and he should honor those who are excellent in an art."[225]

AUTHORITY AND POWER

Leadership, even as an expression of humility (a product of the *serving-leader attitude*), still exercises authority, motivating people to willingly do what has been asked because of personal influence. Authority is different than power, although some leadership literature uses the words interchangeably.[226] Power does come with position, but it can be "two-faced. One face is the use of power...to achieve one's personal goals to the detriment of others... The other [is] to achieve the collective goals...even at the expense of the leader's personal goals."[227] Power can be bought or sold and given or taken. Not so with authority. It is earned because of a person's character as expressed in his/her behavior. Jesus amazed listeners, because "he taught with real authority—quite unlike their teachers of religious law." [228] He did this, not because He tapped into His Deity, but in His humanness. He was totally human, because "he gave up everything [he emptied himself] and became... like one of us."[229] By doing so, He showed us what a wholehearted God-follower could be like.

Jesus Christ has left us with examples of the behaviors of humility that one can follow—even emulate. The result of His humble authority is still being felt today. It is a great paradox that in the Kingdom of God is the walk of humility that leads to glory. As Jesus pointed out when little children were gathered around him, "So anyone who becomes as humble as this little child is the greatest in the Kingdom of Heaven."[230]

Self-adulation (gathering glory for self) may be a track to power for some leaders, but at the end of that tunnel one doesn't find the light of authority. Instead, one may find a train bent on wreaking havoc to those powering along and not paying attention. One may achieve power, but have very little influence or authority with honor. Fully implementing the *serving-leader attitude* determines how well the leader handles the giving and receiving of honor. We all like honor. Sometimes, it comes with the position we hold. Sometimes, it comes because of the authority we acquire and how well we influence others. It is the self-talk that no one sees that may be the greater problem, because, when honor is given and we receive it to ourselves only, we are like the person who tries to pick up a slippery watermelon seed. Once you get your fingers around it and think you have it, it slips away. So it is with honor and humility. If we think it is ours, it slips away. We are created to "glorify God" and that includes giving Him any honor bestowed on us. This does not mean some public display of piety; it simply means one's self-talk focuses on thanking God for the encouragement and giving it back to Him, since He is the source for our success.

LISTENING WITH HUMILITY

You know that look from the person who "has it all together?" It's a proud look. Sometimes it's a glance. A smirk. A roll of the eyes. A look that says, "How in the world could you ever be that dumb?" God's Word specifically warns us about this: "*These six things the Lord hates, indeed, seven are an abomination to Him: a proud look [the spirit that makes one overestimate himself and underestimate others].*"[231] That is a jarring reminder that The Lie began the process that produces arrogance because of pride. The Lie of the Serpent has resulted in humanity rejecting what God said and seeking what *man* says. The "look" that says "I know better" is always born of arrogance.

It's a look that should never cross a leader's face. But it does sometimes. Pride is like that—insidious. Authentic, inspirational leadership does not underestimate others. Connecting to the team demands that leaders be vulnerable. In their September/October 2000 *Harvard Business Review* article "Why Should Anyone Be Led By You?" Goffee & Jones talk about four qualities of inspirational leaders. One of those qualities is that leaders selectively show their weaknesses: "by exposing some vulnerability, they reveal their approachability and humanity."[232]

How does the leader become vulnerable without being unduly exposed?

- First, the leader must authentically lead wherever he or she is—work, play, home—because leading is a state of being. One is not the leader because of a position. Just because someone rises to the top does not make one "a leader." The path to the top may have nothing to do with leadership.
- Second, attitude plays a key role: "do nothing from factional motives [through contentiousness, strife, selfishness, or for unworthy ends] or prompted by conceit and empty arrogance. Instead, in the true spirit of humility (lowliness of mind) let each regard the others as better than and superior to himself [thinking more highly of one another than you do of yourselves]."[233]

The authentic leader's attitude is to be fully human, vulnerable and approachable. This takes "courage," but not some manufactured 'courage' because of past achievements, current success, or the prideful belief that s/he can accomplish anything. I'm talking about courage that has its basis in faith and trust that God is good and gracious and wants the best for you—no matter the circumstance. This is powerful stuff that is difficult to reconcile with the hard-charging spirit of the times. Still, the leader who is open to the thoughts of others—their experiences, knowledge, and words of wisdom—will truly achieve this Biblical mandate.

A young, vital, talented and impressive business friend of mine moved to Oregon about the time my wife and I transitioned from California to Oregon. Gordon Viggiano and I had lost contact with each other when I left San Jose and moved to San Diego (before our move to Oregon), but we reconnected in Oregon and soon after, at the age of 51, Gordon suffered a stroke. As he puts it, "I have a hole in my head."[234] Life, as it had been experienced for Gordon and his family changed—dramatically. But as Gordon tells his story, he challenges us.

> *Things happen to everyone. We all have, or will have, obstacles to overcome. But what do we do when those obstacles are so big, they block ALL our light? How do we find our footing when **everything** we know, **everything** we rely on, **everything** that makes us feel secure, is lost in the dark?*
>
> *I am here to tell you... that kind of darkness is thick with fear. Together with my family, we had to do two things: first, we had to learn to not be afraid of the dark; and, second, we had to find our way back to the light. The long journey from then to now has been filled with many emotions and challenges.*[235]

His story is important for all of us. I hope you will have the opportunity to experience Gordon and Jill sharing their story. But of interest to us (in this section of developing a *serving-leader attitude* by learning to give of yourself with humility) are Gordon's insights as a result of his stroke, which has left him with some right-side paralysis (affecting the use of his right arm), speech difficulties, and loss of some mental acuity. But Gordon at 70% is still more insightful, wittier, more determined, more disciplined and more gracious than many of us at 100%.

His insights include the following:

> *When this crisis came along, we had the 'opportunity' to find out what our faith really means to us. **Everything** we held as normal, **every** plan we had made, **every** routine we were used to was **gone**. Our future was completely unknown. We had to find out what it really means to put God first and live on faith...*
>
> *You know, I don't think you have to have a stroke to struggle with insecurities. Perhaps you are challenged physically, emotionally, financially, professionally. How will you face these challenges? Are you willing to fight through fear, failure and*

uncertainty? Will you let them define you and paralyze you, or can you learn from them and become more?

Maybe you don't think you have the right equipment. Maybe, like me, you think "I might fail" or "I don't look right" or "I am not the person I used to be." Maybe you think "I'm too old" or "I'm too young" or "I'm too inexperienced" or "I'm not smart enough" or...the list goes on. Regrettably, standing still is so much easier than moving forward. I don't know why building confidence is so hard while eroding it is so easy. But I do know this: if you listen to your negative self-talk, you will soon believe it!

Taking that first step

*Maybe taking that first step is a little overwhelming. Perhaps you need to learn how to ask for help. If you are like I used to be, asking for help was worse than falling into the darkness! I believed if I worked hard enough, I would find the solutions. I thought I could climb **any** mountain by myself. How foolish of me.*

Pride

Pride can certainly be a heavy weight to carry around. It makes the getting up so much harder. Now that I have a hole in my brain, asking for help is a necessity. And guess what? It's not so bad! People like to help! Even people who would never return my calls when I had my swagger have now made time for me and offered encouragement.

We all have something we need, and we all have something to give. We can make each other's lives meaningful. A little grace, a little generosity, a little patience, and a little encouragement can go a long way. Today, you may be the giver of these things. Tomorrow, you may be the receiver. There are blessings to be had on both sides. No one climbs Everest alone. No one wins an Olympic medal without help.

I am obviously far from perfect. I have only one functioning carotid artery supplying blood to my brain. I am more fragile in my overall health, but I am in training, and I invite you to train with me. After all, aren't we all trying to climb a mountain or win a gold medal? While some people's mountain actually is Mt. Everest or even Mt. Hood, yours can be as personal as mending a relationship or starting a new career. You're going to experience setbacks and disappointment, but you will also experience excitement and achievement!

Always remember: it's not about falling down; everybody falls down. **It's about getting up**—*no matter how many times it takes."*[236]

Gordon's story, this chapter on humility, and the seventy questions in this book all will be in vain if you still are trusting in yourself to fulfill your basic needs—let alone learning to know yourself, control yourself and show up in all your relationships as humble. Never forget to "give all your worries and cares to God, for he cares about you."[237] Your struggles in answering the questions may cause you to "fall down" with discouragement, dismay, negative self-talk, and distraction. Remember Gordon's words: "Everybody falls down. *It's about getting up*—no matter how many times it takes."

I close with the words of our Creator, who willingly became human, who reminded His disciples and us to remember these incredible truths.

"What I'm trying to do here is get you to relax, not be so preoccupied with getting so you can respond to God's giving. People who don't know God and the way he works fuss over these things, but you know both God and how he works. Steep yourself in God-reality, God-initiative, God-provisions. You'll find all your everyday human concerns will be met. Don't be afraid of missing out. You're my dearest friends! The Father wants to give you the very kingdom itself."[238]

CHAPTER 12 QUESTIONS

Questions 66: In what ways can you seek to meet the needs of others before your own needs? Give specific examples.

Questions 67: How do you (or will you) develop work and communication habits so the team around you shines?

How will you be intentional about supporting this attribute so that when the team does well the team gets the credit, and when the team does poorly you take responsibility?

Questions 68: How do you consciously make room for other egos? How do you (or will you) demonstrate by your actions that you don't know it all?

Use the three attributes of Morris, et.al. cited in this chapter to help frame your thinking.

Questions 69: How will you seek bright people to fill your knowledge and/or expertise gaps?

Questions 70: How will you exercise humility—a sense of holiness—without judging and trying to control others?

Section V:
MAJOR THEORIES OF LEADERSHIP

"There is nothing more difficult to take in hand, more perilous to conduct, or more uncertain in its success, than to take the lead in the introduction of a new order of things."

Niccolo Machiavelli

Over the centuries, a number of theories of leadership have been proposed. I have listed most of them, but am certain I have left a few out (finite and fallible human nature being what it is). Below each theory are my general comments about the focus of each.

GREAT MAN THEORY

Leadership is a product of how you are wired—you are a born leader. You lead when it is demanded. This theory was expounded during a time when the aristocracy ruled, and it was assumed that breeding led to leaders.

It is hard to imagine that this type of leader would be driven to adopt a *serving-leader attitude*. It is the extraordinary leader, when "bred" with the mantle of leadership, who adopts the characteristics that define the behavior of the "others first" attitude.

TRAIT THEORY

A form of the Great Man Theory: leaders are born with the "right" set of traits and skills. Research seems to deduce there is a preferred set of each.[239] These sets of traits and skills, when applied through a *serving-leader attitude* screen, may actually produce positive results; however, you will note there is little focus on others in either set.

TRAITS	SKILLS
• Adaptable to situations	• Clever (intelligent)
• Alert to social environment	• Conceptually skilled
• Ambitious and achievement-oriented	• Creative
	• Diplomatic and tactful
	• Fluent in speaking
• Assertive	• Knowledgeable about group task
• Cooperative	
• Decisive	• Organized (administrative ability)
• Dependable	
• Dominant (desire to influence others)	• Persuasive
	• Socially skilled
• Energetic (high activity level)	
• Persistent	
• Self-confident	
• Tolerant of stress	
• Willing to assume responsibility	**Stogdill (1974)**

BEHAVIORAL THEORIES

The prime driving thought is that leaders are made, not born. Look at what leaders actually *do*—the skills they develop—and learn from them. Both models could be shaped by developing a robust *serving-leader attitude.*

Role Theory Leadership is based on expectations of personal roles and can be shaped by what others expect. The Leadership Style then becomes a predicate of the role team members place on them.[240]

The Managerial Grid Leaders have two concerns: one is for the people, and the other is for the tasks. In the 1960s, Blake & Mouton developed their model of behavioral leadership using a 9 x 9 graph [below is my representation] that presented styles of management their research seemed to indicate.[241]

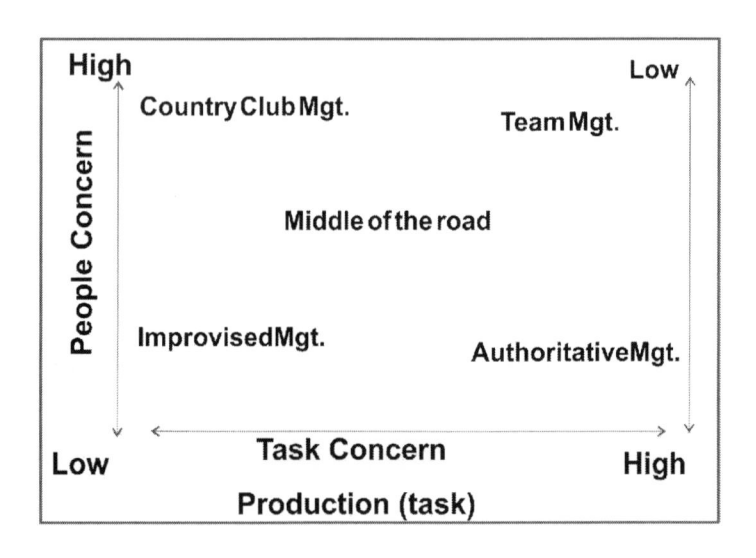

PARTICIPATIVE LEADERSHIP

The theory behind participative leadership models purports that people like to be part of the decision-making process as orchestrated by the leader. These models bode well with the attributes of one who practices leadership with a *serving-leader attitude (SLA)*. Certainly Lewin's Democratic leader and Likert's Consultative and Participative styles could be adopted while maintaining an *SLA*. However, Lewin's laissez-faire style may not fare well with this attitude, considering that the person utilizing a *serving-leader attitude* "meddles" in the life of those being led, albeit to act in their best interest.

Lewin's Leadership Styles—Kurt Lewin (1939) experimented with the leader's decision-making process and determined there were three styles: *Autocratic* (not at all participative), *Democratic* (involves people in the decision-making process), and *Laissez-Faire* (the leader has a hands-off approach and allows the people to make decisions for which they will be held accountable). [242]

Likert's Leadership Styles—Likert's theory goes deeper than Lewin's. Rensis Likert posited there were four decision-making styles: *Exploitive* (fear-based, threatening top-down decision-making), *Benevolent* (concern for people is added to the authoritative style—rewards are part of the process—but it remains, after input, top-down), *Consultative* (open style to listening and asking opinions, but, in the end, the leader makes the final decision), and *Participative* (the leader and the follower work together with minor decisions made at lower levels and major decisions made with participants involved in the process).[243]

SITUATIONAL LEADERSHIP

At the beginning of this book, I posited that one of the two drivers of leadership is context, and it seems, both by experience and research, that the best styles of leadership accurately reflect the situation: the leader is shaped by a range of situational factors. This situational approach assumes that decisions are complex and impacted by external factors along with the internal belief-systems of the leader and participants. Each of the following styles is well received by practitioners and academics alike, and they each fit the *serving-leader attitude* model well. Hersey and Blanchard's model assumes that the leader knows self well (maturity), is able to control responses to situations and therefore able to lead, as the situation demands. That leadership is expressed by "telling and directing" with humility and "delegating and observing" with controls. Self-interest is managed for the good of the team.

> *Hersey and Blanchard's Situational Leadership*—the authors of *One Minute Manager* developed a model based on the belief that leaders change their style dependent on the team's maturity level—what they called "development style." They constructed four styles to match four development styles, which posit that followers move along a continuum from low competence and low commitment to high competence and high commitment. As they move from left to right (low to high), the leader also moves from telling/directing to delegating/observing. [244]

> *Vroom and Yetton's Normative Model*—these authors assumed that, given the situation, if the leader can inspire decision acceptance, there is not only more commitment on the part of the followers, but also more effective action. An *SLA* would posit that inspiration and acceptance are more easily achieved within the paradigm of the others-centered attitude.

They posited five strategies for their model:

1. The leader takes what is known and then alone makes a decision.
2. Leaders work with followers, as a unit, to get information from them, but then they decide alone.
3. Leaders work with followers individually, share problems that need clarification (information), listen to the individual's ideas, but, once again, make a decision alone.
4. Leaders share the problems facing them with followers as a group, use strategies to listen to the group's solutions, and then they decide alone.
5. The leader shares the problems facing the leader with followers as a group, and then works for a consensus agreement, which the leader accepts.[245]

House's Path-Goal Theory of Leadership—was developed to help describe a supportive situational leader (who, however, has a clear sense that there is a right way of getting stuff done) who is focused on the needs of the followers. Certainly this model reflects the major tenants of a *serving-leader attitude*, but the caution is that these supportive behaviors may only be generated by mental habits and not heart changes. When leading only form head knowledge and not heart transformation, danger lurks. People yearn for authenticity. Authentic people are centered and do not just practice certain Pavlovian behaviors from the head, but he or she believes in the behaviors and applies those attitudes and actions to oneself as well as others. They model what they want to encourage. The idea was that effective leaders encourage and support their team to help them achieve the firm's goals in the following ways:

1. Making the path to a solution clear—pointing to the goal the leader wants achieved either directly or with a general hint of the direction;

2. Helping the followers by removing roadblocks that only a leader can remove or by helping a follower move self-imposed road blocks; and,
3. By rewarding followers as they make progress with either intentional encouragement or a clear set of (financial) rewards for achievement.[246]

CONTINGENCY THEORIES

In general, these theories assume that one's ability to lead is contingent on a host of situational factors coupled with the leader's preferred style of leadership and the general capabilities of the followers. These theories all assume that there is no one best way of leading and that the situation determines what approach the leader takes.

Fiedler's Least Preferred Co-worker (LPC) Theory—is based on his identification of how leaders prioritize between tasks and people and how well they can assess others. His research led to a belief that what we think about other people drives the leadership style we might choose. His conclusion was that the approach is dependent on three factors:

1. Leader-Member Relations, referring to the degree of mutual trust, respect and confidence between the leader and the subordinates.
2. Task Structure, referring to the extent to which group tasks are clear and structured.
3. Leader Position Power, referring to the power inherent in the leader's position itself.

What might be important here is that this model assumes the leader can assess others through a "screen" that is not broken, twisted or filled with the leader's own belief system (for example, we may see in others traits we don't like, because they remind us of something in us we don't like).[247]

Cognitive Resource Theory—assumes that one's experiences and native intelligence are factors in a leader's success, yet they are not significant enough to predict success—because stress is a game-changer and impacts the ability of a leader to make decisions. This model posits three possibilities (at minimum):

1. That a leader's "cognitive ability" determines when a leader chooses to be directive or facilitative.
2. Recognition that stress changes everything. For example, an intelligent person who has honed rational skills may seek a rational explanation when one is not available, and the stress of that futile seeking mitigates the cognitive ability naturally present.
3. That a leader's experience can ameliorate the effect of stress on decision-making and enable a leader to react in a positive way. Of course, this assumes the leader has *learned* from the results produced when stress inhibited the ability to use brain-power to problem solve. Experience may be a good teacher but only if one *learns* from that experience.

Note: Fiedler linked his work to this theory.

Strategic Contingencies Theory—was developed by D. J. Hickson, et.al. in 1971, and posits that power within an organization depends on three characteristics:

1) One's ability to solve problems (and those people are *always sought out*);
2) Being active in the critical path of the stuff that needs to get done within an organization; i.e., one is very visible and solves problems well; and,
3) One's personal uniqueness—bringing a certain level of skill that makes one difficult to replace.[248]

TRANSACTIONAL LEADERSHIP

Generally, this leadership model assumes a clear chain of command, where reward and punishment are used as motivational tools and the primary purpose of the chain is to make sure subordinates understand that their purpose is to do what the person above them has told them to do. Success is *contingent* upon results and on how well the transactional leader creates clear command and control structures. These leaders seem to generally manage by *exception*—meaning, if the follower is exceptional, he or she is rewarded, but if the subordinates produce results that don't meet the rule or expectation, they are held responsible (despite not having the resources or capabilities needed), and "punishment" of some sort follows.

This kind of leadership is limited, in my opinion, because it assumes that humans are controlled by simple external motivations. I see this theory of "leadership" to be less about leading and more about managing.

Leader-Member Exchange (LMX) Theory—describes the dynamics of leaders in groups driven by a tacit understanding of the relationship the leader maintains with group members. This theory notes there exist *in-groups* (the inner circle members who *pay* for this special relationship in the currency of work, commitment and loyalty) and *out-groups* (whose members have little influence in the organization). The leader needs to nurture the relationships with the "ins" while limiting the power granted in a manner and method so a *coup* does not occur—a real balancing act for the leader.[249]

FIGURE 1

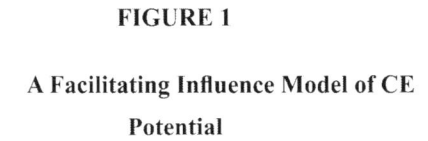

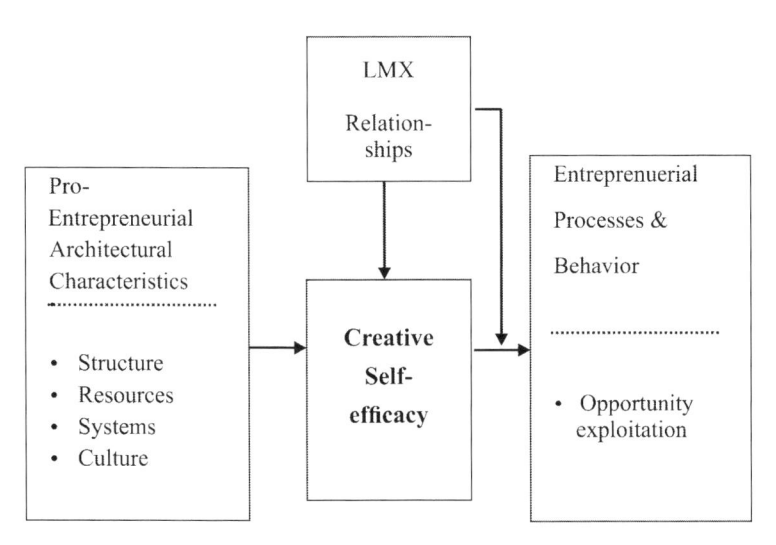

A Facilitating Influence Model of CE Potential

```
                    ┌──────────────┐
                    │    LMX       │
                    │ Relation-    │
                    │ ships        │
                    └──────┬───────┘
                           │
┌─────────────────┐        │          ┌──────────────────┐
│ Pro-            │        │          │ Entreprenuerial  │
│ Entrepreneurial │        │          │ Processes &      │
│ Architectural   │        ▼          │ Behavior         │
│ Characteristics │   ┌─────────┐     │                  │
│                 │──▶│ Creative│────▶│ • Opportunity    │
│ • Structure     │   │  Self-  │     │   exploitation   │
│ • Resources     │   │efficacy │     │                  │
│ • Systems       │   └─────────┘     │                  │
│ • Culture       │                   │                  │
└─────────────────┘                   └──────────────────┘
```

LMX certainly centers attention on the interaction of the leader and the follower. Is this a transactional exchange or a transformational exchange? That question is still open for debate, although some recent scholarship has found that, done well, it is more transformational, especially in organizations where an entrepreneurial spirit is rewarded. Figure 1 below illustrates this process. [250]

TRANSFORMATIONAL LEADERSHIP

This model assumes people follow those who inspire them with vision and passion and a shared enthusiasm and energy to make stuff happen. It also assumes the leader really does care for the followers, wants them to succeed, and wants them to become leaders.

The promise of transformation occurs at two levels. The first is the leader's promise to change the firm (ah, but here is the rub: if the firm is seeking not transformation but status quo, a natural tension exists). Notwithstanding the organization's current status, implied in the transformation is that the people will also be transformed—another product of the process. Vision setting and selling are critical factors for the leader to consider.

Bass' Transformational Leadership Theory—B. M. Bass defines this in terms of how well a leader *transforms* followers who admire, respect and ultimately trust the leadership skills of their leader. He suggests that followers may be transformed when...

1. They understand the value and importance of what they do;
2. They learn to focus on the firm's goals and objectives rather than their personal goals; and
3. They move from basic *needs* into a higher-order of need (purpose, for example).

The leaders who can transform authentically are those who have a strong moral foundation grounded with ideals that influence, motivation that inspires, intellect that stimulates and a strong consideration for *others*.[251]

Burns' Transformational Leadership (TL) Theory—As defined by J. M. Burns, this theory is different from Bass in that Burns sees TL as a mutuality process—where both the leader and the follower work to help each other raise the bars of morality and motivation. Burns sees TL as a highly collaborative process that incorporates social and spiritual values and drivers of motivation—connecting people with a higher purpose, yielding a search for meaning and identity and attracting people to the values of both the leader and the follower.[252]

Kouzes and Posner's Leadership Participation Inventory—Kouzes and Posner are developers of a survey (The Leadership Practices Inventory) that resulted in a list of preferred characteristics of leaders (over a period of twenty years, more than 75,000 people were interviewed).

The list, in order of importance is as follows:

- Honest
- Forward-looking
- Competent
- Inspiring
- Intelligent
- Fair-minded
- Broad-minded
- Supportive
- Straightforward
- Dependable
- Cooperative
- Determined
- Imaginative
- Ambitious
- Courageous
- Caring
- Mature
- Loyal
- Self-controlled
- Independent

The results of their work include five actions they have identified as being key for successful leadership:

- **Model**—Live out the behavior you expect people to adopt. What you do is more important than what you say.

- **Inspire**—People are inspired when ideas capture their imagination, and especially when the ideas follow from a vision that is effectively communicated, which grows the people and the business.
- **Challenge**—Difficult situations and adversity are the main food on which effective leaders thrive. They want innovation, which is often the product of challenging "the way it has always been done."
- **Enable**—Encouraging people is not enough. Leaders must enable followers to put their ideas into action, and the followers must feel that their ideas have value.
- **Encourage**—Passion from the heart is unleashed when the leader taps into the enthusiasm of the followers, resulting in people who behave their best, because they are passionate about what they do and why they do it.[253]

7 TRANSFORMATIONS OF LEADERSHIP[254]

Although the work of David Rooke and William Torbert does not rise to the level of a *leadership model*, I've included it here, because their article—"7 Transformations of Leadership" in the April 2005 edition of *Harvard Business Review*—stuck with me. There are two reasons. The first was the subhead to the article, which states, "Leaders are made, not born, and how they develop is critical for organizational change." The second reason was their list of seven traits and their profiling percentages (Opportunist—5%; Diplomat—12%; Expert—38%; Achiever—30%; Individualist—10%; Strategist—4%; and Alchemist—1%). The last two were most interesting for their potential, but highly under-utilized according to their research sample. They characterized the Strategist as a person who is transformational by recognizing the power of team members and empowering them through sharing visions that are both organizational and personal in nature. They encourage inquiry. They support personal transformation—themselves first, and others next—as a means of being successful change agents. Although I don't believe in using the word "evolve" because of its implications, I do agree with their assessment that "those who are willing to work at developing themselves and becoming more self-aware can almost certainly evolve [adapt and change—my words] over time into truly transformational leaders."[255]

Brazeal's newest book[256] certainly demonstrates that transformation is possible—especially to those who have had hearts regenerated by the Living God.

ROSOFF—THE PROTEAN LEADERSHIP MODEL

Dr. Rosoff developed a model based on her view that seven paradoxes of leadership require conscious effort on the part of leaders to make choices that will result in organizations managing complexity in uncertain times. ("Protean" means versatile, adaptable, changeable, inconsistent, and even fickle.)

Her research yielded the following relationships:[257]

The Protean Leadership Model		
Paradoxes	*Leadership Capabilities*	*Conscious Actions*
Connection	Integrity	Deep Relationships
Decision-making	Accountability	Own Your Decisions
Growth	Embrace Ambiguity	Manager Complexity
Static Organization	Continuous Learning	Find Hidden Leaders
More	Good Judgment	Minimize Greed
Search for Meaning	Humility	Become Meaningful
Purpose	Life Balance	Serve a Larger Purpose

TRANSCENDENTAL LEADERSHIP THEORY

A recent movement in leadership literature suggests there is a fourth "T" in the leadership train from Trait, to Transactional, to Transformational, to the newest, Transcendental.

This latter category is a macro-theory under which a *serving-leader attitude* fits as a model of behaviors that link the leader to the follower in a way that is more holistic than simply inspirational and motivational. The linkage suggests there must be an element of spiritual perspective that is different in tone and texture than the normal organizational focus placed on the first three T's—one that is more concerned about "wholeness" not only of the person, but also of the organization. That wholeness of the organization, by extension, could be applied to the community, the culture, and ultimately the world.[258][259][260][261]

GREENLEAF—SERVANT-LEADERSHIP

First introduced by Robert K. Greenleaf, and often dismissed in leadership literature of the 1970s and 1980s, this is now a recognized form of leadership for American businesses and suggests that leaders focus on the needs of followers to achieve their leadership goals.

Subsequently, many writers have developed leadership models evoking the servant-leadership sentiment. The more well-known writers include Warren Bennis, Ken Blanchard, Stephen Covey, Max DePree, William Pollard, Peter Senge and Margaret Wheatley. Peter Northouse and Glenn Rowe both include chapters in their leadership textbooks on the Servant-Leadership Model. The newly emerged servant-leader characteristics are listed earlier in this book. Those expounded by Greenleaf[262] include the following:

- Initiative of the Individual
- Listening and Understanding
- Acceptance and Empathy
- Awareness that is Greater than Conscious Reality
- Foresight and Conceptualization
- Persuasion
- Healing and Serving—Commitment to Others
- Creating Community
- Trustee and Stewardship

Both sets of behavior may be practiced without a changed heart and may mislead some, who believe that by being "good" and practicing these behaviors they make themselves good enough for life with God. We can never make ourselves good enough for God. It takes a heart changed by God Himself to make us acceptable to Him.

BIBLIOGRAPHY

Ariely, D. (2012, May 26). Why We Lie. *Wall Street Journal*, p. C1 & 2.
Baldoni, J. (2009, September). *HBR Blog Network*. Retrieved April 10, 2012, from http://blogs.hbr.org/baldoni/2009/09/humility_as_a_leadership_trait.html
Bennis, W. G. (1994). *An Invented Life: Reflections on Leadership and Change.* New York: Perseus-Basic Books.
Berger, L. (2011). *The Talent Managment Handbook: Creating a Sustainable Competitive Advantage by Selecting, Developing, and Promoting the Best People.* New York: McGraw-Hill.
Bingham, D. J. (2002). *Pocket History of Church.* Downers Grove: InterVarsity Press.
Blanchard, K. (2002). *Whale Done! The Power of Positive Relationships.* New York: The Free Press.
Bowman, R. W. (1957). *The Gospel From the Mount: A New Translation and Interpretation of Matthews, Chapters 5 to 7.* Philadelphia: The Westminster Press.
Brazeal, D. (2011). *THE NEW BUSINESS PARADIGM: A Christian's Worldview in a Secular Marketplace.* Amsterdam: Creative Storytellers NL.
Bridges, J. (2008). *Holiness Day by Day.* Colorado Springs: NavPress.
Burns, J. M. (1978). *Leadership.* New York: Harper & Row.
Christensen, C. M. (2010). How Will You Measure Your Life? *Harvard Business Review*.
Collins, J. (2001). *Good to Great.* New York: HarperCollins Publishers.
Collins, J. & Porras, J. (1997). *Built to Last: Successful Habits of Visionary Companies.* New York: HarperCollins.
Crosby, P. B. (1996). *The Absolutes of Leadership.* San Francisco: Jossey-Bass Publishers.
Dauten, D. (1996). *The Max Strategy: How a Businessman Got Stuck at an Airport and Learned to Make His Career Take Off.* New York: William Morrow and Company.
DePree, M. (1992). *Leadership Jazz.* New York: Dell Publishing.
Dickson, J. (2011). *Humilitas: A Lost Key to Life, Love, and Leadership.* Grand Rapids: Zondervan.
Drucker, P. F. (2004). What Makes an Effective Executive. *Harvard Business Review*, Reprint R0406C.
Freska, M. (2009). *Traces of the Atlantic Civilization.* Print-on-demand Publishing: Pluramon, via www.lulu.com.
Gardiner, J. (2006, Spring). *Transactional, Transformational, and Transcendent Leadership: Metaphors Mapping The Evolution of the Theory and Practice of.* Retrieved from Leadership Review: http://www.leadershipreview.org/2006spring/Article3.pdf
Gill, D. W. (2004). *Doing Right: Practicing Ethical Principles.* Downers Grove: InterVarsity Press.

Girzone, J. F. (1987). *Joshua: A Parable for Today.* New York: Scribner.
Greenleaf, R. K. (2008 (1970)). *The Servant as Leader.* Westfiled: The Greenleaf Center for Servant Leadership.
Harkavy, G. W. (2004). *Leading Turnaround Teams.* St. Charles: ChurchSmart Resources.
Heathfield, S. M. (n.d.). *about.com.* Retrieved from Susan M. Heathfield: http://humanresources.about.com/od/rewardrecognition/a/recognition_tip.htm
Heifetz, R. A. (1994). *Leadership Without Easy Answers.* Boston: Harvard Univserity Press.
Hill, A. (2008). *Just Business: Christian Ethics for the Marektplace.* Downers Grove: InterVarsity Press.
Hunter, J. C. (1998). *The Servant: A Simple Story About the True Essence of Leadership.* Rocklin: Prima Publishing.
Hussey, D. S. (2012). *Does Prayer Create Integration Between Intuitive and Logical Decision-Making Processes for the Christian Business Leader? A Grounded Theory Examination.* Minneapolis: Capella University.
Jaust, D. G. (2008, September 6). The University's Crisis of Purpose. *New York Times.*
Jenson, R. (1989). *The Bible in Business.* Sisters: Questar Publishers.
Johnson, D. (2001). *The Transparent Leader.* Mecanicsburg: Executive Books.
Johnson, J. J. (2012, March). Genesis Critics Flunk Forensic Science 101. *Acts & Facts*, 8-9.
Jones, L. B. (1995). *Jesus, CEO: Using Ancient Wisdom for Visionary Leadership.* New York: Hyperion.
Kellerman, B. (2010). *Leadership: Essential Selections on Power, Authority, and Influence.* New York: McGraw Hill.
Keller, T. (2008). *The Reason for God.* Hieleah: Dutton.
Kotter, J. P. (1990). *A Force for Change: How Leadership Differs From Management.* New York: The Free Press.
Kotter, J. P. (1996). *Leading Change.* Boston: Harvard Business School Press.
Kotter, J. P. (1998). What Leaders Really Do. *Harvard Business Review: Leadership Insights*, 52.
Kouzes, J. & Posner, B. (1987). *The Leadership Challenge: How to Get Extraordinary Things Done in Organizations.* San Franciso: Jossey-Bass.
Lencioni, P. (1998). *The Five Temptations of a CEO.* San Francisco: Jossey-Bass.
Lencioni, P. (2000). *The Four Obsessions of an Extraordinary Executive.* San Francisco: Jossey-Basss.
Lengel, R. L. (2000). *Fusion Leadership: Unlocking the Subtle Forces That Change People and Organizations.* San Francisco: Berrett-Koehler.
Lewis, C. S. (1961). *The Screwtape Letters.* New York: Macmillan.
Liu, C. (2007, June 2). *Transactional, Transformational, Transcendental Leadership: Motivation Effectiveness and Measurement of Transcenden-

tal Leadership. Retrieved from http://www.udel.edu/: http://www.ipa.udel.edu/3tad/papers/workshop6/Liu.pdf

Lucas, J. R. (1997). *Fatal Illusions: Shredding a Dozen Unrealities That Can Keep Your Organization From Success.* New York: ANACOM.

MacDonald, G. (2003). *Ordering Your Private World.* Nashville: Thomas Nelson.

Manning, B. (2005). *The Ragamuffin Gospel.* Colorado Springs: Multnomah Books.

Mansfield, S. (2007). *Ten Tortured Words: How the Founding Fathers Tried to Protect Religion in America...and What's Happened Since.* Nashville: Thomas Nelson.

Meyer, R. S. (2002). *The Five Pillars of Leadership.* Tulsa: Oklahoma.

Morris, J. A. (2005, October). Bringing Humility to Leadership: Antecedents and Consequences of Leader Humility. *Human Relations,* pp. 1323-1350.

Mouw, R. J. (1992). *Uncommon Decency: Christian Civility in an Uncivil World.* Downers Grove: InterVarsity Press.

Northouse, P. G. (2013). *Leadership (Sixth Edition).* Thousand Oaks: Sage.

Paglia, C. (2012, November). Beauty. *Smithsonian,* pp. 11-12.

Pearcey, N. R. (2004). *Total Truth: Liberating Christianity From Its Cultural Captivity.* Wheaton: Crossway Books.

Pearcey, N. R. (2010). *Saving Leonardo: A Call to Resist the Secular Assualt on Mind, Morals, & Meaning.* Nashville: B&H Publishing Group.

Peck, M. S. (1978). *The Road Less Traveled.* New York: Touchstone.

Perkins, B. (2011). *The Jesus Experiment: What Happens When You Follow in His Footsteps?* Carol Stream: Tyndale House Publishers.

Peters, T. (1985). *A Passion for Excellence.* New York: Random House.

Pollard, C. W. (2005). *The Heart of a Business Ethic.* Lanham: Universtiy Press of America.

Robinson, B. (2009). *Incarnate Leadership.* Grand Rapids: Zondervan.

Rooke, W. R. (2005). 7 Transformations of Leadership. *Harvard Business Review,* 67-76.

Rosenbach, W. E. (2012). *Contemporary Issues in Leaderhip.* Boulder: Westview Press.

Rosoff, N. (2011). *The Power of Paradox: The Protean Leader and Leading in Uncertain Times.* New York: Routledge.

Rowe, W. G. (2013). *Cases in Leadership.* Thousand Oaks: SAGE.

Sanford, D. (2008). *If God Disappears: 9 Faith Wreckers & What to Do About Them.* Carol Stream: TYNDALE.

Schenkel, M.; Brazeal, D.; & Maslyn, J. (2009). Corporate Entrepreneurship: The Facilitating Effects of Creative Self-efficacy and Leader-Member Exchange. *The Southern Journal of Entrepreneurship - 2,* 1-23.

Segan, C. (1980). *The Cosmos.* New York: Random House.

Sharma, R. S. (1997). *Leadership Wisdom from the Monk Who Sold His Ferrari.* New York: Haper Collins.

Siler, T. (1999). *Think Like a Genius: The Ultimate User's Manual for Your Brain.* New York: Bantam Books.

Singer, D. S. (2011). *Start-up Nation: The Story of Israel's Economic Miracle.* New York: Hachette Books.

Skarlicki/Gilliland/Steiner. (2003). *Emerging Perspective on Values in Organizations.* Greenwich: Information Age Publishing.

Sproul, R. (1971). *Reason to Believe.* Grand Rapids: Zondervan Publishing House.

Sproul, R. (2011). *St. Andrew's Expositional Commentary: 1-2 Peter.* Wheaton: Crossway.

Stephens, S. (2004). *21 Surprisingly Simple Steps to a Great Life.* Wheaton: Tyndale House.

Stogdill, R. M. (1974). *Handbook of Leadership: A Survey of Theory and Research.* New York: Free Press.

Tuttle, W. (2005). *World Peace Diet: Eating for Spiritual Health and Social Harmony.* New York: Lantern Books.

Viggiano, G. (2012, April 10). My Brain Has a Hole In It! Lake Oswego, Oregon, USA: Unpublished Manuscript of a first-person presentation.

Warren, R. (2002). *Purpose Driven Life.* Grand Rapids: Zondervan.

SCRIPTURE INDEX

Old Testament

Genesis 1:26-27	82
Genesis 2:7	81, 82
Genesis 3:6	81
Genesis 4:7	33
Leviticus 19:9	44
Leviticus 22:31	70
Numbers 14:24	138
Joshua 3:7	148
Nehemiah 8:10	110
Esther 4:14	35
Job 2:3 ,9	45
Psalm 119:36	54
Proverbs 1:5	91
Proverbs 2:2	36, 52
Proverbs 2:9	52
Proverbs 4:20-23	86
Proverbs 6:16-17	151
Proverbs 10:11	109
Proverbs 10:25	21
Proverbs 11:3a	45
Proverbs 12:1	106
Proverbs 12:18	111
Proverbs 12:26	144
Proverbs 13:3	111
Proverbs 14:8	61
Proverbs 15:2	96, 97
Proverbs 15:23	108
Proverbs 15:24	55
Proverbs 15:31-32	103
Proverbs 16:11	71
Proverbs 17:16	88
Proverbs 17:22	119
Proverbs 21:16	72
Zechariah 4:6	50

New Testament

Matthew 6:22-23	12
Matthew 7:29	150
Matthew 12:50	8
Matthew 15:18	86, 107
Matthew 16:15	22
Matthew 18:4	150
Matthew 20:28	21
Matthew 22:36	136
Matthew 22:37-39	5
Matthew 25:23	33, 121
Mark 8:36	36
Luke 7:30	31
Luke 9:48	143
Luke 11:41	117
Luke 12:15	107
Luke 12:29-32	155
Luke 16:10	47
John 3:8	4
John 3:30	137
John 4:24	82
John 6:33	9
John 14:6	8
John 14:24	11
Acts 13:22	79
Romans 1:25	83
Romans 6:13	137
Romans 12:10	148
Romans 12:11	130
1 Corinthians 2:14	82
2 Corinthians 5:17	45
2 Corinthians 10:5	86, 107
2 Corinthians 13:5	33
Galatians 6:4	34
Ephesians 3:16-19	12

Ephesians 4:2	24
Ephesians 4:22-23	85
Ephesians 6:7	139
Ephesians 6:12	140
Philippians 2:2-8	147
Philippians 2:3	152
Philippians 2:5	147
Philippians 2:7	150
Philippians 4:6-7	136
Philippians 4:8	86
Colossians 1:27	15
Colossians 2:3	50
Colossians 3:2	85
Colossians 3:12	118
1 Thessalonians 5:18	144
1 Timothy 6:6	107
2 Timothy 1:6	136
2 Timothy 1:7	71
2 Timothy 3:16-17	14
1 Peter 2:13	113
1 Peter 2:20	44
1 Peter 5:7	155
2 Peter 1:2	23
2 Peter 1:3-8	22-24
2 Peter 3:5	68
1 John 5:11-12	12

GENERAL INDEX

5

5 M's of Motivating 149

A

A, B, C's of Constructive Passion 132
Absolutes of Leadership 112
Antecedent conditions 109
Apostle Paul .... 137 - 141, 147-148
Aristotle 9, 21, 67, 79, 82, 91, 101
Authority and Power 150

B

Baldoni, John 145
Bass, B. M. 168
Behaving ethically 6, 44
Bennis, Warren 43, 44, 174
Blake & Mouton 160
Blanchard, Ken 162, 174
Blanchard/Hershey 96, 164
Brazeal, Deborah 118, 122, 129, 171
Buddhists 10
Built to Last 34, 145
Burns, J. M. 168
Burns, Robert 32
Burns' Transformational Leadership 168

C

Cain	33
Caretaker	112
Character-building	72, 109
Christ-centered	69
Christian perspective	5, 6, 72, 110
Christians	8 - 10, 41, 46, 65, 130
Cicero	131
Cognitive Resource Theory	165
Collins, Jim	34, 103, 144, 145
Collins/Porras	34
Communication	20, 28, 82, 96, 97, 99, 109, 112, 121, 126, 156
Conceptualizing	6
Constructive passion	132, 133, 134
Contentment	107
Contingency Theories	21, 164
Controlling self	4, 23, 79, 106
Coolidge, Calvin	65
Covetousness	107
Covey, Stephen	174, 200
Creating value	6, 111, 112
Crosby, Philip	112

D

Democratic: Leadership Styles	161
Dependable: Leadership Practices	169
DePree, Max	174
Descartes	9, 131
Destructor	112
DISC profile	28

E

Effective leaders	20, 31, 69, 92, 93, 96, 110, 138, 146, 163, 170
Emery, Stewart	120
Emotional healing	4, 34, 109, 125
Empowering	6, 125, 171
Erasmus	8
Ethic(s)	12, 22, 23, 41- 55, 72, 105
Exercising control	23
Exploitive: Leadership Styles	161

F

Fair-minded: Leadership Practices	169
Fiedler's Least Preferred Co-worker (LPC) Theory	164
Foresight	93, 94, 95, 174
Forward-looking: Leadership Practices	169

G

Giving self	4, 23,
Goffee & Jones	151
Good to Great	103, 145
Graham, Martha	130
Great Man Theory	158, 159
Greed	54, 107
Greenleaf	6, 45, 46, 93, 174

H

Harley-Davidson	119
Harmonious passion	132
Healing	6, 34, 109, 111, 112, 114, 125, 174
Heathfield, Susan	119
Hegel, G.W.F.	131
Heifetz, Ronald	111
Helping	19, 120, 121, 125, 133, 135, 164
Hickson, D. J.	165
Hill, Alexander	53, 103
Honor	50, 87, 147, 148, 150, 151
House's Path-Goal Theory of Leadership	163
Humility	14, 17, 24, 52, 86, 118, 121, 143,-155, 156, 162

I

Inspiring: Leadership Practices	170
Integrity	45, 46, 51, 81, 87, 96, 130
Intelligent: Leadership Practices	170
Introspection	27, 31, 32, 39

J

Job	45, 46, 51, 62, 67, 73, 91, 94, 110, 121, 122
Jones, Laurie Beth	50, 94
Joshua	138, 148
Joy	33, 108, 110, 114, 137
Justus von Liebig	95

K

Kant, Immanuel 105
Keller, Helen 137
Keller, Tim 42
Kepler, Johannes 88
Kotter, John 18, 110, 120
Kouzes and Posner's Leadership Participation Inventory 169

L

Laissez-Faire: Leadership Styles 161
Lao Tsu 102
Lazarus, Frank 31
Leader-Member Exchange (LMX) Theory 166, 167
Leadership skill 168
Leadership Without Easy Answers 111
Leading .... vii, 7, 9, 11, 14, 18, 21, 28, 29,
   32, 36, 42, 45, 47, 50, 51, 54, 58, 63, 64, 66, 85, 101, 111, 118, 122,
   123, 129, 133, 139, 152, 163, 164, 166
Lengel, R. L. 6, 19
Lewin, Kurt 161
Lewin's leadership styles 161
Lewis, C. S. 13, 46
LIFO 28, 98, 122, 133
Likert, Rensis 161
Likert's leadership styles 161
Lombardi, Vince 17
Lowry, Colonel John 119
Loyal: Leadership Practices 169

M

MacDonald, Gordon 83
Machiavelli 150, 157
Mallory, Susan 51
Managing 4, 18, 34, 51, 64, 83, 133, 166, 172
Managing From the Heart 19
Managerial Grid 160
Mature: Leadership Practices 169
Meyer and Slechta 125, 138
Model: Behavior 169
Morris, Andrew 146
Motivation(s)...13, 20, 24, 109 110, 112, 117-125, 132, 149, 166, 168, 169, 173 150, 168, 170, 171
Muslims 10

N

Northouse 174

O

Obedience 11, 54, 147
Obsessive passion 132
One Minute Manager 162
Openness 146

P

PACE profile 28
Paglia 9
Participative Leadership 161
Passion(s) .... 23, 24, 95, 118, 129 - 141, 149, 150, 168, 170
Passionate .... 21, 129, 135, 137 - 139, 141, 170
Pearcey, Nancy 65, 68, 70, 84, 146
Peck, M. Scott 106
Penn, William 36
Peters, Tom 130
Plato 9, 67, 68, 91, 104, 138, 201
Pollard, William 174
Porras, J. 34, 120
Praise 83, 86, 120-122, 125
Preparers 112
Procrastinators 112
Proficiencies 23, 91, 97
Protean Leadership Model 172
Purpose 5, 8, 12, 15, 18, 22, 23, 31-34, 36, 38, 41, 43, 44, 51, 52, 63,
    64, 66, 67, 68, 73, 75, 82, 88, 103, 107, 118, 129, 134, 138, 141, 166,
    168, 169
Putting followers first 6

R

Relationship(s) 4, 7, 8, 10,-12, 15, 16, 36, 38, 42, 46, 63, 72, 82, 97, 105,
    106, 111, 112, 118, 135, 136, 155, 166, 172
Role Theory 160
Rooke, David 171
Rosoff, Nina 35, 172
Rowe, Glenn 174

S

Sagan, Carl 65, 68
Sanford, David... 49
Self-awareness... 12, 28, 32, 101, 146
Self-controlled: Leadership Practices 169
Self-discipline 31, 102, 106
Self-talk 51, 94, 107, 124, 151, 154, 155
Selling 137,168
Senge. Peter.. 174
Servant-leadership............................... 5, 6, 18, 19, 34, 109, 174
Serving-Leader Attitude™ .... 4, 5, 7, 8, 11, 12, 14, 15, 17, 18, 19, 20, 21, 31, 32, 33, 34, 35, 36, 37, 41, 44, 45, 46, 47, 49, 50, 51, 52, 53, 54, 55, 61, 66, 71, 83, 84, 85, 88, 91, 95, 96, ,97, 102, 106, 107, 109, 110, 112, 117, 120, 121, 123, 125, 130, 132, 133, 136, 138, 139, 144, 146, 147, 148, 149, 150, 151, 153, 158, 159, 160, 161, 162, 163
Sharing visions 173
Siler, Todd 95
Situational Leadership.. 19, 96, 162
Smalley/Trent 28
Socrates.. 9, 21, 27, 31, 41, 61, 104
Spartacus 125
Sproul, R. C. 44, 105, 112
Straightforward: Leadership Practices....................................... 169
Strategic Contingencies Theory... 165
Stress 88, 97, 102, 165
Supportive: Leadership Practices.................................... 163, 169

T

Tabula rasa... 104
The Great Commandment... 5, 136
The Leadership Practices Inventory... 169
The Lie 47, 55, 69, 151

The New Business Paradigm 118
The Road Less Traveled 106
Think Like a Genius 95
Thompson, Mark 120
Trait Theory 59
Transactional Leadership 168
Transcendence 146
Transcendental Leadership 173
Transformational Leadership .... 3, ,6, 12, 19, 21, 123, 167, 168, 171, 173
Transformative 6, 10, 35, 66
Trusting environment 124
Truth ...... vii, 7 - 10, 14, 15, 19, 33, 41, 42, 43, 46 - 51, 54 - 56, 58, 62, 65, 66, 69, 71, 72, 83, 88, 119, 145, 146, 155
Tuttle, Will 44

U

Uniqueness 165

V

Vallerand & Houlfourt 132
Viggiano, Gordon .... 152 - 155
Vision setting 168
Vroom and Yetton's Normative Model 162
Vulnerable 151, 152

W

Warren, Rick 5
Whale Done 124
What Leaders Really Do 120
Wheatley, Margaret 174
Wilson Learning 28
Winthrop, John 69
Worldview.......... 12, 23, 45, 61, 62, 63, 65, 66 - 73, 74, 75, 103, 118, 129, 146, 147

Z

Zacharias, Ravi 49

ENDNOTES

[1] John 3:8 NIV
[2] (Rosoff, 2011), pp. 156-192
[3] (Warren, 2002), p. 17
[4] Matthew 22:37-39 CEV
[5] Writers like Bennis, Blanchard and Hodges, Covey, DePree, Pollard, Gill, Senge, and Wheatley.
[6] (Lengel, 2000), p. 176
[7] By Liden, Wayne, Zhao, Henderson and Meuser.
[8] I do realize that theologians would say "immanent" (as the Divine manifesting a presence in the material world), but I'm assuming that my readers are not necessarily theologians, and "closeness" is the meaning I'm seeking, thus my choice.
[9] John 14:6 NIV
[10] (Bingham, 2002), p. 106
[11] (Bingham, 2002), p. 106, quoting Erasmus, *The Handbook of the Christina Soldier,* fifth rule, in *The Erasmus Reader,* ed. E. Rummel (Toronto: University of Toronto Press, 1990), p. 152.
[12] Matthew 12:50 NIV
[13] John 6:33—the link http://biblos.com/john/3-33.htm will help yield understanding about the Greek text.
[14] In 1983, Holmes wrote a book by that title and still may be available at Amazon.com.
[15] (Paglia, 2012), p. 12
[16] John 14:24 TLB
[17] Ephesians 3:16-19 CEV
[18] 1 John 5:11-12 CEV
[19] Matthew 6:22-23 CEV
[20] (Lewis, 1961), p. 38
[21] 2 Timothy 3:16-17 NIV
[22] (Deuteronomy 17:14-20; 1 Kings 19:3-18; Proverbs 16:19; 25:6,7; Luke 14:7-11; Luke 16:15; Romans 12:3)
[23] (Rosenbach, 2012), Rainer Niermeyer, as quoted by Becker, p. 247
[24] (Rosenbach, 2012), p. 247
[25] Colossians 1:27 NIV
[26] (Sproul, 2011), p. 93
[27] (Kotter, 1996), pp. 25-30
[28] (Lengel, 2000), p. 178

[29] Proverbs 10:25 NIV
[30] Matthew 20:28 NLT
[31] 2 Peter 1:3-8 CEV
[32] Matthew 16:15 CEV
[33] 2 Peter 1:4 CEV
[34] 2 Peter 3:4 CEV
[35] 2 Peter 3:5 CEV
[36] 2 Peter 3:5 CEV
[37] 2 Peter 3:1 NIV
[38] 2 Peter 1:1 AMP
[39] 2 Peter 1:5 NIV
[40] 2 Peter 2:6 NIV
[41] Ephesians 4:2 NIV
[42] 2 Peter 2:6 NIV
[43] 2 Peter 2:7 NIV
[44] 2 Peter 2:7 NIV
[45] Plato posited that truth could only be found through rigorous self-examination. Confucius said, "I examine myself three times a day. When dealing on behalf of others, have I been trustworthy? In intercourse with my friends, have I been faithful? Have I practiced what I was taught?"
[46] Luke 7:30 NIV
[47] (Rosoff, 2011), reporting Lazarus on p. 129
[48] 2 Corinthians 13:5 NIV
[49] (Lencioni, 2000), pp. 15-16
[50] Robert Burns, *Poem "To a Louse"—verse 8: Scottish national poet (1759-1796)*
[51] Genesis 4:7 NLT
[52] Matthew 25:23 NIV
[53] Galatians 6:4 AMP
[54] (Collins, J. & Porras, J. 1997), p. 224
[55] Esther 4:14 NIV
[56] (Rosoff, 2011), p. 119
[57] Dr. Del Tackett used these terms in *The Truth Project*.
[58] Westminster Shorter Catechism
[59] Mark 8:36 NIV
[60] http://quotationsbook.com/quote/8361/
[61] Proverbs 2:2 NLV

[62] Pastor and author Tim Keller quoted in Gospel Coalition, www.thegospelcoalition.org
[63] United States of American Declaration of Independence, partial quote of the first sentence.
[64] (Keller, 2008), pp. 276-276
[65] (Bennis, 1994), p. 23
[66] (Tuttle, 2005), p. 11
[67] Leviticus 19:9, 13b NLT
[68] (Sproul, 2011), p. 83
[69] 1 Peter 2:20 NKJV
[70] (Lengel, 2000), p. 188
[71] Proverbs 11:3a NKJV
[72] Job 2:3 NKJV
[73] Job 2:9 NLT
[74] (Greenleaf, 2008), (1970), p. 15
[75] 2 Corinthians 5:17 NIV
[76] (Ariely, 2012), p. C1
[77] Luke 16:10 NIV
[78] (Ariely, 2012), p. C2
[79] (Mansfield, 2007) has done an exhaustive study of the nature of our Founder's view of religion in America and the dismantling of what was intended by the Framers of the First Amendment.
[80] (Sanford, 2008), p. 38
[81] (Sanford, 2008), p. 39, quoting Ravi Zacharias, *A Shattered Visage* (Grand Rapids: Baker House, 1990), p. 136
[82] Colossians 2:3 NASB
[83] Zechariah 4:6 NIV
[84] (Gill, 2004), p. 60
[85] (Rosoff, 2011), quoting Susan Mallory, President of Northern Trust's Southern California Region, p. 126
[86] This is difficult to do: I have failed to keep my eyes fixed, and I understand that if I want to produce the results written about, I must practice daily the basic spiritual disciples of study, mediation and prayer.
[87] Westminster Shorter Catechism
[88] Proverbs 2:2 NASB
[89] Proverbs 2:9 NKJV
[90] (Hill, 2008), p. 64

[91] (Christensen, 2010), Reprint R1007B.
[92] (Pollard, 2005), pp. 33-56—my points were chosen from his discussion of "The Tao" that C. S. Lewis developed in his book *The Abolition of Man*—Tao represents for the Western mind the Law of Nature.
[93] Psalm 119:36 TLB
[94] Proverbs 15:24 NLT
[95] Proverbs 14:8 NIV
[96] A great book to read about the loss of religion in America is *Ten Tortured Words* by Stephen Mansfield.
[97] (Johnson, 2012), p. 9
[98] (Sagen, 1980), p. 1
[99] http://physics.about.com/od/classroomphysics/ig/Washington-DC-science-sites/NAS.htm
[100] Dr. Del Tackett does a marvelous job of developing an understanding of the use of this artwork as an example of the battle between those who look at the universals vs. those who look at the particulars for meaning in life.
[101] A philosopher before Socrates, who believed that the universe was always changing, is famous for his observation that no person ever dips their foot in the same river twice. He applied that concept of the ever-changing to his view of life, the universe and the idea that everything has an opposite property.
[102] 2 Peter 3:5 KJV
[103] (Stephens, 2004), p. 11
[104] The evolutionary perspective is that this "god" developed by the evolving *homo sapiens* to create an external "crutch" to support attitudes and behaviors that generally benefit society.
[105] Leviticus 22:31—treating God as Common and Ordinary is warned against.
[106] 2 Timothy 1:7 NLT
[107] Proverbs 16:11 AMP
[108] Proverbs 16:11 MSG
[109] Proverbs 21:16 NIV
[110] Acts 13:22 NIV
[111] http://dictionary.reference.com/browse/congruent
[112] http://www.mathopenref.com/congruentaas.html
[113] Genesis 2:7 NIV

[114] Genesis 3:6 NIV
[115] Genesis 3:6 NIV
[116] Genesis 2:7 NIV
[117] I Corinthians 2:14 NKJV
[118] Genesis 1:26-27 NIV
[119] John 4:24 NIV
[120] Romans 1:25 NIV
[121] (MacDonald, 2003), p. 32
[122] (Pearcey, 2010), p. 277
[123] (Pearcey, 2010), p. 277, quoting J. Gresham Machen
[124] Ephesians 4:22-23 NLT
[125] Colossians 3:2 NIV
[126] 2 Corinthians 10:5 NIV
[127] Philippians 4:8 CEV
[128] Matthew 15:18 MSG
[129] Proverbs 4:20-23 MSG
[130] Proverbs 17:16 NLT
[131] Proverbs 1:5 NASB
[132] (Drucker, 2004), Harvard Business Review, June 2004, reprint R0406C
[133] (Drucker, 2004), p. 1
[134] (Jones, 1995), pp. 62-64
[135] (Jones, 1995), p. 63
[136] (Siler, 1999), p. 193
[137] Proverbs 15:2 NKJV
[138] Proverbs 15:2 NLT
[139] Founder of Taoism which, "as a political philosophy, can be considered in contrast to Confucianism. Whereas the latter is concerned with rules and rituals, the former is more elusive, more mystical, and more paradoxical." (Kellerman, 2010), p. 3
[140] (Kellerman, 2010), p. 5
[141] Proverbs 15:31-32 NLT
[142] (Collins, 2001), p. 138
[143] Hill, p. 138, quoting Kateregga and Shenk.
[144] A very interesting exploration of the historical and archeological evidences of vast cultures destroyed by a "great deluge" of water may be found in German historian Martin Freska's book, *Traces of the Atlantic Civilization*. Although I do not agree with all his conclusions regarding

dating of times, periods and epochs, his gathering of historical research about ancient, no longer existing civilizations, supports the Biblical text. I believe it demonstrates that the world "that once was" (as Apostle Peter 2 Peter 3:6) was advanced in technology, even beyond today's advances and was characterized by vile, sinful behaviors.

[145] (Sproul, R. C., 1971), pp. 148-149
[146] (Sproul, R. C., 1971) from which I have summarized some of his thinking about Kant's perspectives on behavior and justice.
[147] Proverbs 12:1 AMP
[148] Proverbs 12:1 NLT
[149] (Peck, 1978), p. 15
[150] 2 Corinthians 10:5 NIV
[151] Matthew 15:18 NIV
[152] Luke 12:15 NLT
[153] 1 Timothy 6:6 NIV
[154] Proverbs 15:23 AMP
[155] Proverbs 10:11 NKJV
[156] (Northouse, 2013), p. 225
[157] See Colossians 3:5 NIV
[158] (Kotter, 1990)
[159] *"Now is the winter of our discontent, made glorious summer by this sun of York"* are the opening words of the play, Richard the III, by William Shakespeare.
[160] Nehemiah 8:10 NKJV
[161] Proverbs 12:18 MSG
[162] (Heifetz, 1994), p. 184
[163] (Crosby, 1996), pp. 9-25
[164] Proverbs 13:3 NLT
[165] (Sproul, R. C., 2011), *1 Peter*, p. 78
[166] 1 Peter 2:13a NIV
[167] This is a reference to a once-held belief that life started with chemicals being stimulated by an electric charge—a bolt of lightning as it were. Numerous, unsolvable problems exist with that theory that are not discussed in textbooks or popular literature about life. For those interested, this article may be of some help: http://www.icr.org/article/evolution-hopes-you-dont-know-chemistry-problem-wi/
[168] Luke 11:41 TLB

[169] Colossians 3:12 MSG: However, the Amplified has a more instructive rendering to consider: "Clothe yourselves therefore, as God's own chosen ones (His own picked representatives), [who are] purified and holy and well-beloved [by God Himself, by putting on behavior marked by] tenderhearted pity and mercy, kind feeling, a lowly opinion of yourselves, gentle ways, [and] patience [which is tireless and long-suffering, and has the power to endure whatever comes, with good temper]."

[170] (DePree, 1992), p. 7
[171] (Brazeal, 2011), p. 138
[172] (Brazeal, 2011), p. 35
[173] (Singer, 2011), p. 78
[174] Proverbs 17:22 MSG
[175] http://humanresources.about.com/od/rewardrecognition/a/recognition_tip.htm
[176] As quoted from http://www.hesselbeininstitute.org/newsletters/iow/2009/july17.html
[177] Kotter, HBR journal article *What Leaders Really Do*, p. 54
[178] Matthew 25:23 NIV
[179] (Berger, 2011), p. 284—article by Stark and Royal on "Rewarding Your Top Talent"
[180] (Brazeal, 2011), p. 104
[181] (Blanchard, 2002), p. 40 and following
[182] (Meyer, 2002), pp. 108-109
[183] Refer to the list in Chapter 1 of this book for the seven behaviors of a servant-leader.
[184] (Lengel, 2000), p. 174
[185] (Brazeal, 2011), p. 70
[186] (Peters, 1985), p. xx
[187] (Lucas, 1997), p. 169
[188] (Sharma, 1997), author of *The Monk Who Sold His Ferrari*, quoted at http://www.leadershipdevelopment.com/html/article1.php?art_id=150 from Sharma's "Reflections on the Rituals of Wise Leaders."
[189] Romans 12:11 NIV
[190] (Jensen, 1989), p. 67
[191] www.brainyquote.com/quotes/authors/m/martha_graham.html
[192] http://plato.stanford.edu/entries/descartes-ethics/

[193] http://www.brainyquote.com/quotes/quotes/g/georgwilhe101479.html#
[194] www.quotationspages.com/quote/29247.html
[195] http://dictionary.reference.com/browse/passion?s=t
[196] (Stephen W. Gilliland, 203), p. 175
[197] Philippians 4:6-7 NIV
[198] Matthew 22:36-40 CEV. "Teacher, what is the most important commandment in the Law?" Jesus answered: Love the Lord your God with all your heart, soul, and mind. This is the first and most important commandment. The second most important commandment is like this one. And it is, "Love others as much as you love yourself." All the Law of Moses and the Books of the Prophets are based on these two commandments.
[199] 2 Timothy 1:6 JB Phillips
[200] John 3:30 TLB
[201] Romans 6:13 MSG
[202] (Meyer, 2002), p. 84
[203] Plato, as quoted Kellerman, p. 19
[204] Numbers 14:24 NIV
[205] Ephesians 6:7 NIV
[206] Toward this end, I highly recommend that you read, study, and apply the biblical principles presented in Sara J. Moulton Reger's outstanding book, *Lead and Succeed* (Excel Books, 2009).
[207] (Lucas, 1997), pp. 167-177 provides an interesting discussion about the force of passion within an organization.
[208] Ephesians 6:12 NIV
[209] Luke 9:48b TLB
[210] (Collins, J. 2001), *Good to Great* is a recommended read to develop a rich understanding of how humility—among other attributes—can be a game-changer when managing any organization.
[211] 1 Thessalonians 5:18 ESV
[212] Proverbs 12:26a NASB
[213] (Baldoni, 2009), Harvard Business Review blog (HBR blog) where John Baldoni, in 2009 this leadership development consultant, executive coach, speaker, and author of ten books wrote a blog about humility–http://blogs.hbr.org/baldoni/2009/09/humility_as_a_leadership_trait.html
[214] (Morris, 2005), pp. 1323-1350

[215] (Pollard, 2005), p. 188—a lecture by Donald G. Soderquist given at University of Southern California in 2001.
[216] (Hunter, 1998), p. 111
[217] (Pearcey, 2010), p. 276
[218] Philippians 2:2b-8 CEV
[219] Philippians 2:5 NIV
[220] Again, I highly recommend that you read, study, and apply the biblical principles presented in Sara J. Moulton Reger's book, *Lead and Succeed* (Excel Books, 2009).
[221] Romans 12:10 NASB
[222] Romans 12:10 MSG
[223] Joshua 3:7 GWT
[224] (Kellerman, 2010), p. 11, quoting Confucius Analects 1.16
[225] (Kellerman, 2010), p. 38, quoting *The Prince*, XXI
[226] (Rowe, 2013), p. 3: Rowe and Guerrero define power as "the potential or capacity to influence others to bring about desired outcomes. We have influence when we can affect others' beliefs, attitudes and behavior."
[227] (Rowe, 2013), p. 4
[228] Matthew 7:29 NLT
[229] Philippians 2:7 CEV
[230] Matthew 18:4 NLT
[231] Proverbs 6:16-17a AMP
[232] http://hbswk.hbs.edu/archive/1710.html.
[233] Philippians 2:3 AMP
[234] (Viggiano, 2012), p. 1: Gordon made a presentation to a select group of friends in the fourth year of his recovery from a life-changing stroke that Gordon experienced in March of 2008. The title of his presentation was <u>My Brain Has a Hole In It!</u> The title reflects Gordon's business history as a focused, articulate, funny sales executive and trainer. His presentation is a testimony to God's grace and goodness and Gordon's will to learn all over again how to talk, walk, and think in new ways and carry himself. It is a testimony to Jill's (his wife) ability to continue to be the mother to their two children while supporting Gordon in his recovery and dealing with all the practical aspects of paying bills, managing medical and rehab appointments—all the nitty-gritty of living. She has done this with grace and beauty that glorifies God and honors her ability to love, unconditionally.

[235] (Viggiano, 2012), p. 3
[236] (Viggiano, 2012), pp.12-13 & 16-18
[237] 1 Peter 5:7 NLT
[238] Luke 12:29-32 MSG
[239] For a more comprehensive Bibliography concerning the Trait approach to leadership, see (Northouse, 2013) pp. 41-42.
[240] For a deeper exploration, consider http://www.springerlink.com/content/q087726g57870536/
[241] Blake & Mouton have published several books about their approach. Consider Blake, R.R. & Mouton, J. S. (1964) (also 1978 and 1985). *The managerial gird*. Houston, Gulf Cost Publishing.
[242] For more information, consider http://psychology.about.com/od/leadership/a/leadstyles.htm
[243] For more background, consider Cartwright, D. & Sander, A. (1960). *Group Dynamics Research and Theory*. Evanston: Row, Peterson. And Likert, R. (1961) *New Patters of Management*. New York: McGraw-Hill.
[244] (Northouse, 2013), pp.120-121 will provide a more comprehensive list of sources.
[245] For more background, consider Vroom, V.H. & Hetton, P.W. (1973) *Leadership and Decision-making*. Pittsburgh: University of Pittsburgh Press.
[246] For a more complete discussion, consider two sources: (Northouse, 2013), pp. 137-160 and (Rose, 2013), pp.176-199.
[247] For more background, consider (Northouse, 2013), p. 136 for a fuller Bibliography.
[248] Developed by D. J. Hickson, C. R. Hinings, C. A. Lee, R. E. Schneck, and J. M. Pennings and published in a scholarly journal, *Administrative Science Quarterly* Vol. 16, No. 2 (Jun., 1971), pp. 216-229 for which you need college or university access rights.
[249] For a more comprehensive discussion, consider (Northouse, 2013), Chapter 8, pp. 161-184.
[250] (Schenkel, 2009), Figure 1 is from this article.
[251] Consider Bass, B.M (1985) *Leadership and Performance Beyond Expectations*. New York: Free Press.
[252] Consider Burn, J.M. (1978) *Leadership*. New York: Harper & Row.
[253] (Kouzes, 1987 and 2002)
[254] (Rooke, 2005), pp. 67-76
[255] (Rooke, 2005), p. 76

[256] (Brazeal, 2011)
[257] (Rosoff, 2011), p. 160
[258] (Hussey, 2012)
[259] (Gardiner, 2006)
[260] (H, 2007)
[261] CHRM posting: http://www.chrmglobal.com/Articles/258/1/Transcendental-Leadership.html
[262] (Greenleaf, 2008) (1970), pp. 9-48

The 70 Questions

Question 1: How would the four types of people discussed in chapter 1—driven by (A) data, (B) harmony, (C) action, and (D) excellence—accomplish various tasks such as analyzing, sharing vision, executing plans, helping, etc.? 30

Question 2: Why do you think you are here on earth? 38

Question 3: What should be written in your obituary? 38

Question 4: What will be your ovation? 38

Question 5: Why does it matter what you think about? 38

Question 6: How has your journey of life shaped you in childhood, education, life experiencess, and relationships? 38

Question 7: What is your life vision (or purpose)? 38

Question 8: How does your personal vision fit with what you are pursuing today? 38

Question 9: How will your personal vision drive or shape you in your place of employment or where you wish to become employed? 39

Question 10: What mission in life are you currently pursuing? 39

Question 11: How does your personal mission fit with what you are doing now? 39

Question 12: How do you practice self-reflection? How are you learning from the results you have produced? 39

Question 13: When faced with a moral dilemma, what is the basis of the ethical framework you use to address that dilemma? 57

Question 14: What are the guidelines you use to make choices involving your decisions and behavior? 57

Question 15: Do you believe that personal truthfulness, accountability and respect for the individual are without variation even in the face of changing circumstances? 57

Question 16: What are your core values? 57

Question 17: How do your values impact others? 58

Question 18: How do you manage moral ambiguities? 59

Question 19: Describe your source for Truth and why you believe it can guide you? 59

Question 20: What role does your ethical framework play in your leading? 59

Question 21: How do your moral choices allow you to help your "team members" define direction? 59

Question 22: What is the impact of a negative moral choice you might make, and what will you do because of it? 59

Question 23: What is the role of your *obligations*? Are they binding or can they be changed? 59

Question 24: In what ways do your moral choices inspire and motivate? 59

Question 25: How do you set expectations for those around you so your values are clearly communicated? 59

Question 26: How do you monitor an inclination to lead from a position of power? 59

Question 27: What are some *practical* ways to "pay attention" to what God teaches rather than to the shifting ethical framework of the world? 60

Question 28: How does your life offer hope to a lost world? 60

Question 29: What is your creation narrative? 74

Question 30: What do you believe is the problem with humans—the human condition? 74

Question 31: How is the human condition solved? What is the "redemptive force" that will change the human condition? 74

Question 32: What is your worldview? 74

Question 33: How does your *worldview* motivate you to live out your core values at home, at work and at play? 74

Question 34: In what ways does your view of the world reflect or reject the current culture? Implications? 75

Question 35: How do you anticipate problems and use your worldview to help ameliorate them? 75

Question 36: After considering your worldview, how does this change your purpose statement? 75

Question 37: After considering your worldview, how does this change your ethical framework and your core values?.......... 75

Question 38: Analyze your day: How much time do you spend on your body, your mind and your spirit? 90

Question 39: How do you make the connections between your body, mind and spirit stronger? 90

Question 40: What process are you developing to "take every thought captive"? 90

Question 41: Do you journal? If not, what process do you use to learn about the results you produce at work, at home and at play? 90

Question 42: What is the most recent non-fiction book have read or are reading? What have you learned that applies to learning to manage or lead?.. 99

Question 43: What is your plan to be a life-long learner? 99

Question 44: What behaviors of yours need to be addressed? 114

Question 45: What tools might you use to help control those behaviors? 114

Question 46: What mental discipline do you need to develop so your words result in joy, hope and inspiration to bring about positive change? 114

Question 47: In what particular ways do you behave that have a healing effect on others? 114

Question 48: How do your particular behavioral/personality strengths impact people in your life? 114

Question 49: How do you create value in your community—and what do you intentionally "give back?" 114

Question 50: What are the negative impacts that may emerge when you use too much of your "strengths"? 114

Question 51: How do you demonstrate that you are committed to clear, consistent, compelling and constant communication about core values and behaviors? 127

Question 52: How do you motivate others? 127

Question 53: How do you intentionally *serve* someone who may look to you as a leader? 127

Question 54: How are you demonstrating inspirational leadership not just in words, but also by consistent actions? 127

Question 55: What specific tools do you use to train others in a way that inspires them? 127

Question 56: How do you align yourself with the culture of a team and contribute fully to it? 127

Question 57: In what specific ways will the tools you use to align, motivate and inspire be supported by Scripture? 127

Question 58: What tools do you use with your team to help guide direction? 127

Question 59: What are some of the most difficult issues you face in applying these tools? 128

Question 60: When you must discipline someone, what are the steps you take to prepare yourself and them? 128

Questions 61: What is your passion? 141

Questions 62: What do you need to do to help you passionately live in the completed future—the "it is so" attitude?........... 141

Questions 63: How will you go about authentically sharing your passion?.. 141

Questions 64: In what ways can you direct your passion to help your "team" be joyful and fulfilled? 141

Questions 65: How are your passion and your purpose connected, and what insights emerge when working on this answer? 141

Questions 66: In what ways can you seek to meet the needs of others before your own needs? Give specific examples.157

Questions 67: How do you (or will you) develop work and communication habits so the team around you shines?............. 157

Questions 68: How do you consciously make room for other egos? How do you (or will you) demonstrate by your actions that you don't know it all? 157

Questions 69: How will you seek bright people to fill your knowledge and/or expertise gaps?.. 157

Questions 70: How will you exercise humility—a sense of holiness—without judging and trying to control others? 157

The 70 Questions | 215

QRC code for LIFO survey:

QRC code for 70 Questions:

Made in the USA
San Bernardino, CA
15 August 2014